THE CREATION OF
MEDIEVAL PARLIAMENTS

MAJOR ISSUES IN HISTORY

Editor

C. WARREN HOLLISTER

University of California, Santa Barbara

THE CREATION OF
MEDIEVAL
PARLIAMENTS

EDITED BY

Bertie Wilkinson
University of Toronto

John Wiley & Sons, Inc.
New York • London • Sydney • Toronto

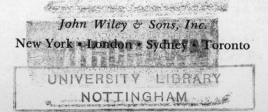

Library of Congress Cataloging in Publication Data:

Wilkinson, Bertie, 1898-   comp.
The creation of medieval parliaments.

(Major issues in history)
Bibliography: p.
1. Europe—Politics—476–1492—Addresses, essays,
lectures.   2. Legislative bodies—Europe—History—
Addresses, essays, lectures.   I. Title.

JN7.W54   328.4'09'02   72-2439
ISBN 0-471-94619-2
ISBN 0-471-94620-6 (pbk.)

Printed in the United States of America

10 9 8 7 6 5 4 3 2 1

To My Family

SERIES PREFACE

The reading program in a history survey course traditionally has consisted of a large two-volume textbook and, perhaps, a book of readings. This simple reading program requires few decisions and little imagination on the instructor's part, and tends to encourage in the student the virtue of careful memorization. Such programs are by no means things of the past, but they certainly do not represent the wave of the future.

The reading program in survey courses at many colleges and universities today is far more complex. At the risk of oversimplification, and allowing for many exceptions and overlaps, it can be divided into four categories: (1) textbook, (2) original source readings, (3) specialized historical essays and interpretive studies, and (4) historical problems.

After obtaining an overview of the course subject matter (textbook), sampling the original sources, and being exposed to selective examples of excellent modern historical writing (historical essays), the student can turn to the crucial task of weighing various possible interpretations of major historical issues. It is at this point that memory gives way to creative critical thought. The "problems approach," in other words, is the intellectual climax of a thoughtfully conceived reading program and is, indeed, the most characteristic of all approaches to historical pedagogy among the newer generation of college and university teachers.

The historical problems books currently available are many and varied. Why add to this information explosion? Because the Wiley Major Issues Series constitutes an endeavor to produce something new that will respond to pedagogical needs thus far unmet. First, it is a series of individual volumes—one per problem. Many good teachers would much prefer to select their own historical issues rather than be tied to an inflexible sequence of issues imposed by a publisher and bound together between two covers. Second, the Wiley Major Issues Series is based on the idea of approaching the significant problems of history through a deft interweaving of primary sources and secondary analysis, fused together by the skill of a scholar-editor. It is felt that the essence of a historical issue cannot be satisfactorily probed either by placing a body of undigested source materials into the hands of inexperienced students or by limiting these students to the controversial literature of modern scholars who debate the meaning of sources the student never sees. This series approaches historical problems by exposing students to both the finest historical thinking on the issue and some of the evidence on which this thinking is based. This synthetic approach should prove far more fruitful than either the raw-source approach or the exclusively second-hand approach, for it combines the advantages—and avoids the serious disadvantage—of both.

Finally, the editors of the individual volumes in the Major Issues Series have been chosen from among the ablest scholars in their fields. Rather than faceless referees, they are historians who know their issues from the inside and, in most instances, have themselves contributed significantly to the relevant scholarly literature. It has been the editorial policy of this series to permit the editor-scholars of the individual volumes the widest possible latitude both in formulating their topics and in organizing their materials. Their scholarly competence has been unquestioningly respected; they have been encouraged to approach the problems as they see fit. The titles and themes of the series volumes have been suggested in nearly every case by the scholar-editors themselves. The criteria have been (1) that the issue be of relevance to undergraduate lecture courses in history, and (2) that it be an issue which the scholar-editor knows thoroughly and in which he has done creative work. And, in general, the second criterion has been given precedence over the first. In short, the question "What are the significant historical issues today?" has been answered not by general editors or sales departments but by the scholar-teachers who are responsible for these volumes.

University of California,
Santa Barbara

C. Warren Hollister

PREFACE

It has been necessary to limit this brief book to a few of the parliaments of medieval Europe and to concentrate on the highlights of their history. Almost every aspect of this subject is a matter of debate, but it has not been possible to do justice to the modern differences of opinion. Some of these differences are revealed in the quotations from modern writers given below, and in general these quotations speak for themselves. They are accompanied by translations of the key records and chronicles, so that the student will be able to form an opinion of his own. General comments on the main problems involved are given at the beginning of each chapter, and an attempt is made to put the history of the medieval parliaments in its proper perspective, as part of the general evolution of medieval society. Finally, a few observations are made concerning works that are likely to be helpful to the student who wishes to pursue his studies further. I am indebted to many writers, and this obligation cannot be expressed in the space at my disposal, but I have made an independent evaluation of some important sources. Throughout I have relied heavily on the judgment of my wife, whose cooperation has never flagged, but the responsibility for errors and omissions is my own.

B. Wilkinson

Toronto, May, 1972

CONTENTS

INTRODUCTION

A study of the creation of the medieval parliament is an examination of the beginnings of our modern democratic assemblies, which now exist throughout the world. It is far more than mere antiquarianism. It teaches us much about the deepest ideals underlying all parliamentary assemblies, often obscured by the complexities of modern life. These ideals are as vital to the democracies of today as they were to the medieval aristocracies.

The emphasis in this study is on the growth of the institution itself, rather than on the coming together of the Estates, in England called King, Lords, and Commons, which ultimately composed it. The origin of these Estates is, indeed, a fascinating problem, going far back into the past; King Alfred divided society into men of prayer, men of war, and men of work, and such distinctions obviously influenced the growth of parliamentary Estates. But they were not responsible for the early acts of creation; these were most frequently initiated by the king and the lords. The essence of the first parliaments was distilled by generations of cooperation between the monarch and the aristocracy. It was the product of a most aristocratic age. The modern preoccupation with the Third Estate, and with representation in the early parliaments, reflects the interest created by modern democracy. This is natural and to be welcomed, but it does not reflect the kind of world in which parliaments began.

The emergence of a recognizable institution, which we may call parliament, occurred in England essentially during the thirteenth century. Most historians are agreed on this point, although there is much difference of opinion about the nature of the assembly that emerged and the changes that preceded it. Bishop Stubbs, still the greatest historian of the English medieval parliament, shows clearly the importance of such questions, and the way in which our answers to them influence our whole interpretation of the process of parliament's creation. He believed that parliament was the great forum where the king and the "nation" cooperated in the highest public affairs. This broad definition took him back to the earliest Anglo-Saxon Witan[1] and forward through the centuries up to the thirteenth, when a new institution was shaped by kings and magnates which gave form to the constitution and through which liberty was preserved. This view was inspired by nineteenth-century liberalism and idealism, although Bishop Stubbs was a Tory, and it has been bitterly criticized. It does, indeed, need to be modified; but its spirit is the one in which to approach the creation of parliament, although it has not been popular in our somewhat negative and unidealistic modern age.

The problems presented by the obscure beginnings of a great institution are not easily solved. One eminent modern historian has been moved to great eloquence by a contemplation of the perils which beset the investigator:[2]

"The mystery which attends on the beginnings of parliament is not peculiar to these particular happenings. It is the mystery which attends on all beginnings, when men are doing things because they are convenient and do not attach conscious significance to them, still less consider what the distant outcome of their acts may be. The word was in the air, the materials were to hand. To track down every nerve in the body politic and locate each impulse, as though they carried some secret message, is as futile as to read into the rivulets which compose the upmost waters of the Thames a foresight of the wharves and shipping in its spacious estuary. Nor should we injure the fragile uncertainties of these beginnings by too eager definition."

Nevertheless, the historian cannot simply turn his back on the problems; and there is both great excitement and a rich reward in attempting to face the difficulties that they present, particularly

[1] See a "Canadian Scholar on the Witan," Chapter I, Document 1 (page 26).

[2] Sir Maurice Powicke, *King Henry III and the Lord Edward* (London, 1947), Vol. I, p. 340. Reprinted by permission of the Clarendon Press, Oxford, England.

when we seek to understand the language of medieval documents
and the obscure motives and forces that underlay them.

Equally dangerous is the attempt to define the place of the
medieval European parliaments in world history. This subject is
so vast and difficult that it has not been discussed in this volume. But two illuminating documents are printed[3] that admirably
reflect the breadth and fascination of the problem. The writers
of both documents—Otto Hintze and A. R. Myers—believe that
the medieval parliaments of Europe represent a unique creation
in world history and can be explained only in terms of unique
political and social conditions. Professor Hintze, in particular,
called attention to three main factors operating throughout Western Europe that are not to be found in the same combination
anywhere else: feudalism, the Church, and a multiplicity of small
kingdoms. Together, Hintze contends, these three factors in-
hibited the growth of royal absolutism so common in other civilizations. Feudalism meant a sharing of political power between
the monarchy and a landed military aristocracy. The Christian
religion and the Church further limited the power of rulers by
continually battling against their claim, explicit or implicit, to
control every aspect of the subject's life. Finally, the development
of many small kingdoms, which by accident or from deeper
causes were never brought together under one ruler, prevented
the rise of an autocratic universal empire. Whether or not we
agree with all of Hintze's suggestions, they show how illuminating the attempt can be to fit the beginnings of parliament into
the framework of world history, and what bright light such spec-
ulation can throw on the problem of origins. The only reason
why I do not pursue the approach at length is that this volume
is only intended to be an introductory essay, in which our primary attention must be given to the limited period when the
medieval parliaments first clearly emerged, and to the individual
manifestation of parliamentary institutions in a limited number
of states.

Both Professor Hintze and Professor Myers recognize clearly
that the differences between the various parliamentary assemblies
were almost as important as their common elements. Indeed, this
point was long ago insisted upon by Bishop Stubbs, in an extract

[3] Documents 1 and 2 (pp. 7–15).

that follows.[4] Many of these differences can be traced to the varia-
tions in political and social organization in different countries.
All historians remark on the exceptional form that feudalism
assumed in England, destined to be the home of the greatest
medieval parliament of all.

Different small kingdoms and a varying feudalism provided the
basic pattern of European political life; but its enduring framework was the Christian Church, and the best way to think of this
society is as a *Respublica Christiana,* which reflects a unity of
faith and culture. Ideas flowed freely from one end of the European world to the other. Among other matters, we may assume
that the problems and conflicts behind the emergence of parliaments were widely known and discussed. The result may be
described as a common political experiment. It is, indeed, remarkable how universal parliaments were within this culture and how
completely absent they were outside.

In developing their parliamentary institutions, men were not
only engaged in struggles for privilege and power, which tended
to be highly localized, but they also were participating in a conflict of principles which was pan-European. The more we recognize that medieval men were as interested in liberty (defined in
their own terms) as we are today, the more we shall agree that
they faced common problems throughout Christendom which they
sought to solve on a basis of common ideas. Parliament was more
than merely a matter of defending special privilege. It was the
supreme medieval instrument for preserving liberty. It was, in the
words of the thirteenth century writer Walter Giffard,[5] a place
for cooperation and reconciliation as well as conflict and con-
frontation. It was not the product of abstract theories of law or of
speculations about political theory, which were rare in the high
middle ages. Instead, it arose out of the age-long habits and traditions of feudalism, with its ideas of personal loyalties, mutual obligations, and limited power. During the thirteenth century, for
example, an outstanding scholar, St. Thomas Aquinas, commented expertly on the *Politics* of Aristotle; but it is doubtful
whether either Aristotle or St. Thomas's comments about him
greatly affected the development of parliament. As Professor

[4] Conclusion, Document 1.
[5] Chapter III, p. 85.

Tierney has concluded,[6] theory tended to follow the event rather than to precede it. In matters of politics, the medieval lord was a pragmatist in the better sense of the term, drawing on the experience of a highly successful society which flourished from the Holy Land to Scandinavia, and applying ancient custom to new problems with ingenuity and common sense. And in nothing was ancient custom more constant and commanding than in the rejection of absolute power.

But parliament was not only the product of ancient custom, it was also the result of, and in part a direct reaction to, institutional, social, and economic progress. Such change alone made parliament possible and, indeed, made its creation necessary if political liberty was to be retained. This creation was part of a vast and complicated development which can very properly be described, in language made familiar by Toynbee, as the response of a whole civilization to a supreme challenge, a response that for good or ill would determine its future life.

The challenge that confronted the men of the thirteenth century was not unique in history. It occurs whenever men, by their creativeness, erect large political structures that produce order and security over a large area, but that consequently tend to shut out the great mass of the community from participation in public affairs. Simple methods of political cooperation become impossible. Government, by its weight and complexity, crushes and destroys the liberty of the individual which it has been created to sustain. The problem this presented had proved to be disastrous to more than one great civilization long before the thirteenth century. Indeed, no enduring answer to it had ever been found. The obstacles in the way of a solution in the Europe of the thirteenth century were, indeed, so formidable that the achievement of one has been described as almost a political miracle. All the protagonists in the constitutional disputes of the age were pioneers faced with the difficulties and uncertainties of a journey into the unknown. Solutions to problems which seem obvious to us now, were then arrived at only through profound controversies, some of which were watered by the blood of martyrs. The new institution of parliament had to be created, as Bryce Lyon has suggested, in a brief moment of history when a precarious balance

6 Document 3.

existed between the forces of order and liberty, and when, in politics as elsewhere, there was a creative spirit abroad that matched the challenge of the times. G. G. Coulton likened the spirit, as it was reflected in architecture, to that of the wonderful moment in a summer dawn when the first light of day grows and broadens upon a world still fresh with all the dews of night.

We are not apt to wax quite so lyrical about mere politics, but perhaps we should. In any case, nothing should be allowed to obscure the sense of crisis and epic struggle which beset the world of the thirteenth century, or the debt which posterity owes to those who undertook the difficult beginnings of parliament. Working without previous models, they created an institution with the potential to solve some of the great political problems of medieval and modern times. We may all be moved by their achievement and by the testimony it offers to the unfailing resources of the human spirit. This is all the more so since we ourselves are engaged in the same endless struggle to reconcile order and liberty, building on their foundations and still adhering to their fundamental ideas.

It seems obvious that, properly approached, the creation of the medieval parliament presents itself as a vast and engrossing problem. It will, indeed, take us far afield. We shall first have to say something about the political implications of feudalism and the way kings and magnates cooperated in a fairly primitive society. We shall look above all at the custom whereby the great lords gave counsel to their ruler as part of their feudal duty; and we shall see that, though this served early kings and lords very well, it became inadequate when feudal kingdoms expanded into territorial states. The old informal relationships which marked the great feudal assemblies gradually became obsolete, and a more formal process of collective agreement was evolved whereby the magnates could participate more fully in decisions which affected all the realm.

Parliament was the institution created to meet the new conditions. We shall examine some of the landmarks in the process of change, noting the diverging paths followed under the influence of differing historical traditions and geographical environments. All these points of resemblance and difference are also to be seen in the growth of representation, which will be the subject of the last chapter. Out of an aristocratic assembly of the king, his "familiars" and his lords, there finally emerged the beginnings of the modern democratic parliament, to which both great forces and great men had made their contribution. The result is writ large over the face of the contemporary world.

1 A German View of the Conditions in World History that Produced Parliamentary Assemblies

[p. 1] The form of government based on representation, which now gives the political life of the whole civilized world its peculiar character, goes back in its historic origin to the medieval Estates-system of government. To a considerable extent this system had its roots, though not everywhere and not exclusively, in the political and social conditions of the feudal system. At least this was so in the most important countries. At many points, indeed, the medieval system of Estates offers a strong contrast of principle to the modern system of representation. Nevertheless, both belong to a single continuous line of historical development. The doubt which has been expressed lately on this point . . . must vanish if we keep in sight the constitutional development of England, for it is hard to see there the boundary line at which the constitution based on Estates changed into the constitution based on representation. We may see this same historical continuity in the French Revolution; and also, with unmistakable clarity, the contrast in principle between an Estates-constitution and the modern order built on representation. For, in the French Revolution, what had been the Third Estate, in the old Estate-order, burst the bonds of the old constitutional arrangement then being revitalized, and made itself the representative of the whole people, the National Assembly.

[p. 4] The question is: how to explain the remarkable fact that Estates and representative constitutions only appear as native

SOURCE. Otto Hintze, "Weltgeschichtliche Bedingungen Der Repräsentativverfassung" (The Conditions in World History necessary for Representative Constitutions), in *Historische Zeitschrift*, Vol. 143 (1930–1), pp. 1–47.

products in the Christian West. Here, apparently, they are to be found fairly generally; in the rest of the world on the other hand, not at all.

In attempting to answer this question we may naturally, in the first place, begin with the two all-embracing systems by which state and society in the West were ruled and characterized: feudalism and the Christian Church, the latter in the shape of the Roman Catholic hierarchy. Feudalism and the Church both contained important and primary motive forces which helped to shape the development of the constitution of Estates. But a third cause was closely associated with them; namely the peculiar mode of state-formation in the West which engendered a constant competition for supremacy in power, without this leading to a process of unification into a universal empire. Precisely because of this competition, European governments expanded their scope of operations and became much more systematic than before. They drew in part on administrative methods inherited from the civilization of Antiquity, and in this the Church played an intermediary role.

As a result of this development, we are confronted by two closely connected phenomena of world history: that of the modern European state-system and that of the modern sovereign state. Both of them in their essential individuality are confined to the Christian West, just as is the Estates-and-Representative constitution; and both phenomena are indigenous there. We may venture to claim that such an Estates-and-Representative order would never have appeared without this particular state-system combined with continual conflict, the latter engendered by rivalry and by the movement of modernisation which accompanied this. The movement made the machine of state more rational and complex. The whole new order can only be fully understood if we grasp its dependence on the structure of European state-life.

[p. 40] The uniqueness of the Estates-system in the West lies precisely in the fact that it is a phenomenon concomitant with a particular form of state-constitution which we find only in the history of the West. Outside the Christian West, as a consequence of the connection between secular and clerical power, state-formation tends towards universal monarchy which at heart favors the rise of absolutism. The deepest factor preventing such a monarchy in the West was the peculiar constitution of the Church and its political activities in opposition to the state. Church-state conflict ensured that the state-system of the West would develop in the direction of a diversity of co-ordinated states which were mutually recognized as being independent of one another. Together, they constituted what, since the sixteenth or seventeenth century, has been called the European state system.

This stage for the organization of the European state followed an earlier one whose outlines appeared as early as the twelfth century. At that time, the states-system was still composed of small, regional polities. It was loose in structure compared with the later system composed of large national states. Yet in spite of this it can be regarded as already a state-system in process of formation, for which the Roman Church provided the framework which held it together.

[p. 46] The growing intensification of the activities of the state, and the consequent strengthening of the factors pertaining to authority and government, now led everywhere to a more or less visible reaction of the corporate spirit against a one-sided strengthening of the institutions of sovereign power. This happened just in the area where the old primitive idea of customary right had maintained some vitality, and where the beginnings of the privileged groups first formed. This reaction eventually gave rise to the establishment of regular constitutions based on Estates. The development took many different courses. In England, feudal absolutism had succeeded in preventing the barons from lapsing into feudal chaos, and in keeping the magnates as a group in the service of the state authority, bound by duty and service. The kings succeeded in drawing the powerful and privileged element among the magnates into the increasing task of vigorous local government. Thus, in the sphere of local administration, there came about a fruitful synthesis of the principles of authority and of the feudal group. In this case, the development of the parliamentary system appears as a progressive centralization of this local machinery of government.

In Poland and Hungary on the other hand, by contrast, elected powerless kings, who were often foreigners, ruled over a more or less highly privileged nobility. The nobles brought ancient regional associations such as the *Wojewodschaften* and *Komitate*

(*comitatus*) into their domain and subjected them to their aristocratic power. On this basis, the system of Estates then grew up
as a kind of republic of the nobility with a monarchical head.

In France and Germany, after the groupings of the nobility
and of the district leaders had broken down, the local administration was reshaped in the spirit of patrimonial rule, and the
princely administrative authority prevailed. In such circumstances,
the group reaction of the nobility found clearest expression in
the development of the system of Estates. Everywhere, the primitive right of resistance (*Widerstandsrecht*) with its barbarously
repressive measures gave way to relatively sophisticated preven-
tive methods of curbing royal power through the co-operation of
Estates. This was exercised in the legislative process, in the granting and administration of taxes by the Estates and their organs,
and in a system of complaints and petitions against the abuse of
princely administrative authority.

Thus the system of Estates developed in its various manifesta-
tions. It provided the prototype of the modern constitutional
systems. Such systems have gradually conquered the whole civilized world. They have culminated in the parliamentary system of
today; though this seems to have entered a period of grave crisis,
through deep changes in the political and social structure of the
world following the great war.

[German]

2   *An English View of Parliamentary*
         Development in Europe

[p. 338] . . . if we see that, in one phase of European development, these older parliaments were almost universal throughout
Latin Christendom and commonly powerful in their functions,

SOURCE. A. R. Myers, "Parliaments in Europe: The Representative Tradition." This article was part II of an essay first published in *History Today*,
Vol. 5 (1955), pp. 383–390, 446–454. Limits of space prevent a longer extract
from this survey, and students are strongly advised to read it for themselves.
Reprinted by permission of the author.

the question naturally arises why this should have happened. Is the explanation simply that this is a stage through which all civilizations pass? This is a problem which has so far not attracted much attention in Britain: but it has aroused the interest of various German historians, especially Otto Hintze and Dietrich Gerhard.

These historians have demonstrated that before the spread of European influence over the rest of the world in the eighteenth and nineteenth centuries, the representative institutions of Latin Christendom were unique. There was no parallel in the absolute monarchies or the city states of the ancient civilizations of the Mediterranean or the Near East. The Aryan invaders of India had a priesthood, a warrior aristocracy, and a peasantry, like the societies of early European civilization; but in the caste-system that subsequently developed in India there was no soil to encourage the growth of representative institutions. There was no room, either, for such a growth in the old China of the fatherly divine authority of the emperor, the bureaucracy of the mandarins, the importance of the family groups, and of conservative custom. Muslim civilization and Japanese culture passed through a phase not unlike that of European feudalism, so that some scholars have used the terms 'Islamic feudalism,' 'Japanese feudalism.' But whereas in Europe feudal society was followed by the flowering of assemblies of Estates, nothing of the kind seems to have happened in Islam or Japan. And striking as this difference is between the culture of Latin Christendom and other civilizations, it is even more remarkable that representative institutions, as Latin Christendom knew them, never developed in Russia. It is remarkable because Russian civilization looked back to Graeco-Roman and Hebrew roots as did that of the West; and if there is the theme of divergence from the West in Russian history, there is also the theme of connexion with it. . . . [p. 388]

Representative institutions . . . [p. 446] arose in thirteenth- and fourteenth-century Europe in monarchies where the prince, representing the unity of the state, and the Estates or Stände, [p. 447] representing the manifold interests within the state, stood over against each other, yet necessarily bound together in one organic body. This duality is a fundamental feature of the states of fourteenth- and fifteenth-century Europe, each side having its rights that the other must respect, neither having the right to control the whole life of the state to the exclusion of the other. If, then, it was ordinarily fundamental to this kind of state—the Ständestaat, as the Germans have succinctly called it—to have a prince (the Swiss Confederation and the North Italian towns were exceptional), a prince who had certain rights but was bound to respect the rights and privileges of others, we have to ask how such a conception of monarchy came to be.

In the beginnings of the history of Western Europe we find one root of this conception in the strong notion among the Germanic peoples, that the king was not an absolute lord, able to do as he pleased with his subjects, but the guardian of custom, and that fealty was binding upon the subject only so long as the king also fulfilled his duty. It is true that this notion was not unique to the early Germanic peoples, as some historians have supposed. It is also true that there was in Germanic kingship another element, pointing towards a very different development—the notion that the king ought to be of the right kin, and that correct blood-relationship to his predecessors, and the correct ceremony of initiation, endowed him with an almost magical efficacy and power. But in the formative centuries of Europe, with their wild disorder and weak government, conditions did not favour the strengthening of the second element, whereas they fostered the development of the first. In Francia the growth of hereditary kingship was stunted by the displacement of the Merovingian dynasty, which had the sanctity of the right kin group, by the Carolingian kings, devoid of any hereditary claims, and therefore driven to stress the rightfulness of their rule and their rôle as guardians of law, order and the church. Though the Church could, and did, exalt the royal authority by the ceremonies of anointing and coronation, which gave the king a quasi-sacred character and taught that he was God's deputy to whom obedience was due as to one appointed by God, there was a price to be paid. Since the time of St. Augustine of Hippo, there had emerged in the Latin Church a distinctively legal, rational, defining tendency of thought—a tendency sufficiently pronounced and distinctive to arouse later the opposition of the Greek Church. This trend had bred the idea that the divine authority of kingship did not mean irresponsible power; on the contrary, it meant that kingly rule was valid only so long as it was exercised in accordance with divine and natural law, of which the Church was the interpreter. And when, in the eleventh century, the militant Gregorian movement developed in the Church, this view of monarchy came to the fore as an influential force in practical politics —justifying the coercion, deposition, or even the death of a monarch whom the Church should deem to have flagrantly defied the laws by which he had been set on the throne. By comparison with the contemporary Byzantine empire, the princes were weak (save in exceptional cases such as England and Sicily), with only a rudimentary administration at their disposal, and were further weakened by the rivalries of the manifold states of Europe; whereas the Church was comparatively independent, its strength increased by its character as a European-wide organization and its growing centralized administration.

This tendency of the Latin Church to stress the subjection of the ruler to law was reinforced by another powerful force of the eleventh and twelfth centuries—that of feudalism. In this attempt to restore some stability and order to societies almost shattered into anarchy by the tumults of the ninth century, elements from both the Germanic and the Roman heritage were fused and sharpened into a conception of the mutual rights and obligations of lord and vassal, each having his rights and duties within a framework of feudal law and custom. As Matthew Paris was later to put it: *sicut subditus domino, ita dominus subdito tenetur.* If the lord should disregard his vassal's rights, then the vassal should have the right of resistance; and in a situation where the military power of a ruler depended, not on a subservient, paid army controlled by a docile bureaucracy, but on a feudal host led by a warrior aristocracy as proud, and collectively as [p. 448] strong, as the monarchy, such a conception of the vassal's rights was a potent one. Where feudalism had struck deep, we often find churchmen combining with feudal vassals to recall the ruler to the remembrance (as they saw it) of his subjection to law, and to his duty of ruling with the advice of his great men, clerical and lay. . . .

[p. 448] But now we have to remember another factor—the freedom of Western Europe after A.D. 1000 from invasion and conquest from without, except on its margins, as in Poland, Hungary, and the Adriatic coast. Here is a striking contrast to the fate of Russia, whose history was profoundly affected by the fact that for over 200 years it was struggling to free itself from the

Mongolian domination of the Tartars. The greater peace and cohesion now possible in Western Europe meant a more fertile soil for the growth once more of royal authority; it meant, also, favourable conditions for a renaissance that provided the technical devices, especially in finance, for fostering more efficient administration, and also a revival of Roman law, which could furnish powerful doctrines for the enhancement of royal authority. But this very tendency to centralization, and the growth of royal power, itself stimulated a limitation in two ways. In the first place, an expanding administration needed greater resources, and stronger governments, with better weapons at their disposal, led, in a culture of separate and rival states, to an era of longer and more expensive wars. This pressing need for greater income came too quickly for princes to have overcome older notions of the rights of subjects, or at any rate of prelates and magnates, to consent or refuse an imposition on their financial resources; and so, in the circumstances, the needs of the princes could only be met by summoning assemblies of their politically powerful subjects, or representatives of those powerful subjects who were too numerous to come as individuals, in order to ask them for grants of taxation to help the prince in his need.

Secondly, the pressure of the expanding monarchies alarmed those groups that were especially powerful into drawing together into associations for self-defence. As a whole there was no practical alternative to organization for group defence; for, in thirteenth-century Western Europe, threatened groups could not escape the pressure by wholesale emigration. It is true that, as is now more clearly understood, there was considerable internal colonization, or intensification of settlement, in various parts of Western Europe, and there occurred about this time the famous German expansion beyond the Elbe. But these developments, important as they were, did not assume a big enough scale to enfeeble the urge towards the kind of defensive association that spread throughout Latin Christendom. Here is another factor differentiating the history of Western Europe from that of Russia, with its expanding eastern frontier. . . . Russian history . . . presents to our enquiry a nobility more mobile than that of the West, never forming provincial or local institutions strong enough to resist the government for long or capable of imparting vitality to a representative assembly. The Russian nobility never

developed a strong sense of corporate loyalty or group rights. . . .
[p. 448] [On the other hand] in Western Europe part of the effective core of assemblies of estates was almost everywhere formed
by a self-armed warrior aristocracy, as [p. 449] conscious of its
rights and its honour as of its duty and its fealty, and which, until at least the fifteenth century, formed the backbone of the
armies that the princes must use. . . .

[English]

3 *An American View of the Relation Between
   Constitutional Theory and Practice*

One of the most familiar platitudes of our textbooks is the
assertion that Western culture was formed from a fusion of classical and Christian elements. It is true of course like most platitudes. But the textbooks do not always emphasize sufficiently that
often the fusion took place in the Middle Ages, and still less that
in the fields of law and government the works of the medieval
canonists played a crucially important role in the whole process.
Yet it could hardly have been otherwise. The canonists were the
only group of intellectuals in Western history who were pro-
fessionally concerned with classical law and with Christian doctrine to an equal degree. They delighted in applying to the papal
office all the exalted language which Roman law used in describing the majesty of the emperor. They called the pope a
supreme legislator whose very will was law, a supreme judge from
whom there could be no appeal, a "lord of the world," "loosed
from the laws." But these same canonists never forgot St. Paul's
reminder that in the Church all power is given "for edification,
not for destruction." Moreover, although they lacked the critical
insights of a modern historian, there was a profoundly historical
dimension to their thought. Gratian's Decretum depicted for the

SOURCE. Brian Tierney, "Medieval Canon Law and Western Constitution-
alism," *The Catholic Historical Review* (Washington, April, 1966) Vol. 52,
No. 1, pp. 10–15. Reprinted by permission of The Catholic University of
America Press, Washington, D.C., U.S.A.

canonists all the ages of the Church's past—and depicted them "warts and all." The misdeeds of several popes who had sinned and erred in former times were recounted in the Decretum and such examples apparently had a sobering effect on the canonists. One of Gratian's texts (Dist. 40 c. 1) suggested that all popes were to be considered holy. The Ordinary Gloss, written about 1215, commented somewhat drily, "It does not say that they are holy but that they are to be presumed holy—until the contrary becomes apparent." The Decretists were fascinated by the potentialities for reform of a papacy wielding vast power but at the same time appalled by the dangers for the Church if all that power should fall into evil hands. They were up against the very nub of the problem of sovereignty. It is easy enough to avoid a despotism if one is content to tolerate an anarchy. The difficult task is to concede to a ruler all the very great powers needed for effective government while guarding against the dangers of arbitrary tyranny.

The canonists' approach to this problem was to seek in the consensus of the whole Christian community, in the indefectible Church guided by the Holy Spirit, norms of faith and order which could define the limits within which the pope's supreme legislative and judicial powers were to be exercised. (The English parliamentary leaders of a later age would set themselves an analogous task in relation to the political community and the limitations of secular kingship.) . . .

It is a complicated task to reconstruct all the constitutionalist elements in the canonists' thought from their voluminous but scattered glosses, and still more complicated to explain in detail how their ideas influenced the growth of secular government. Basically there were two processes at work. Most obviously the canonists offered reflections on the constitutional law of the Church which could and did influence subsequent speculations on the right ordering of the State. But they also formulated a series of doctrines in the sphere of private law which eventually proved of the utmost importance in the growth of representative government although, at first, they had nothing to do with high matters of state. These private-law doctrines again reflected the collegial structure of the medieval Church. Much of the canonists' day-to-day business dealt with the affairs of ecclesiastical com-

munities. They were therefore led to develop an elaborate jurisprudence concerning the representation of corporate groups, the
prerogatives of the head of a juridical society in relation to its
members, and the rights of individual members in relation to the
whole community before such matters began to be discussed as
overt issues of political theory.

Just as in some primitive economies there is a shortage of good
currency, so too in the medieval polity there was a shortage of
good law, especially of constitutional law. When the need for
more sophisticated structures of public law came to be urgently
felt men naturally turned to the legal rules that were already
available in the province of private law—especially in the well-
developed canonical law of corporations—and applied them in
the constitutional sphere also. . . .

Some scholars will think that ideas and ideals have little enough
to do with the growth of governmental institutions. One young
expert has recently observed that, "It did not matter too much
what one or another theorist said. . . ." And, certainly, we could
all agree that, when medieval kings summoned representative
assemblies, they were not normally inspired to do so by protracted
meditations on the subtleties of canonical jurisprudence. Kings
needed help or counsel or money. They wanted assent to their
policies and political support for them. These obvious facts
should indeed receive due emphasis in any institutional history of
the Middle Ages, but it is a delusion to suppose that, by merely
calling attention to them, we are providing a sufficient explanation for the rise of medieval constitutionalism. The problem of
maximizing assent to governmental policies arises for all rulers
in all societies. It is not normally solved by the development of
representative assemblies. Our argument is not that hard-headed
medieval statesmen behaved in such-and-such a way because some
theorist in a university had invented a theory saying that they
ought to do so. The argument is rather that all men behave in
certain ways in part at least because they adhere to certain ways
of thinking. No doubt the ideas that are most influential in
shaping actions are ones that the agent is hardly conscious of at
all—he takes them so much for granted. But the historian has to
make himself conscious of those ideas if he is to understand the
men of a past age and the institutions that they created. The

works of the medieval canonists provide invaluable source material for the constitutional historian precisely because they can
help him to become aware of the implicit presuppositions about
man and society that lay below the surface of medieval political
thought and political action.

CHAPTER I

THE EARLY FEUDAL ASSEMBLIES

Parliament began in the great assemblies which were summoned by all the feudal rulers of Europe during the generations following the break-up of the Carolingian Empire in the ninth century. Such assemblies already had a long history going back to the early Visigothic, Frankish, and Anglo-Saxon period. Feudalism itself was a whole new way of life. Its growth was a continuous process after the Germanic Invasions; but it developed most conspicuously in the days of the Viking and Arab attacks during the ninth and tenth centuries. These attacks, by destroying the Carolingian Empire, forced European society to reorganize on a regional basis. Along with the feudal fief we see also the first adumbration of later kingdoms, in France and England and even Germany. Feudalism is often condemned as static and chaotic; but in truth it provided not only military strength in those long years of crisis, but also a social and economic framework which sustained recovery and provided growing prosperity.

By the eleventh century, there had arisen in Europe one of the most creative civilizations ever to be recorded. It is true that in its hierarchic order feudalism bore strong marks of its struggle for survival, both in the privileges and power of its nobility, and in the heavy burden borne by the peasants who formed the broad basis of the agrarian economy. Its poverty and violence are well known. Yet they should not be allowed to obscure the simple and obvious sources of its strength.

One such source was the notion of reciprocal obligations which at least in theory bound the great lord as much as the humble peasant. The lord had far-reaching rights which he could enforce against the peasants, with justice or injustice; but he had also obligations towards the peasants, even if these could easily be ignored.

Above all, he owed his dependents protection from violence, and with it the rule of law. Similar reciprocal obligations bound the king to his tenants-in-chief, and also bound these vassals to those who held lands from them. Every relationship was in a sense contractual, to be broken only in extreme circumstances, as when a vassal, who was denied justice by his lord, could solemnly withdraw his allegiance by an act of *Diffidatio*. Such ideas could not control the rough injustices of society; but they were reinforced by strong Christian teachings which constantly upheld the dignity of the individual man.

In addition, the individual was sustained by the life of the group, whose cooperation permeated every level of society. Medieval life was group life in a way that is now difficult to understand. A man never stood alone. Fellowship and neighbourliness helped all ranks to survive in a hard world. Indeed without common action in the group, medieval civilization might have survived, but it would hardly have progressed.

Not the least important of the ingredients necessary for such common action were discussion, counsel, and some kind of consensus. The lowliest villagers discussed together when they should sow and reap; and, when in 1265, those of Peatling Magna in England opposed a king's officer out of sympathy with Simon de Montfort, they had assuredly taken counsel together and arrived at a common decision. The ingredient of counsel can be seen in incidental references of all kinds, as when the poet and mystic William Langland gives us a tiny vignette of village life in the fourteenth century:[1]

> *And thus was a marriage arranged in*
> *the case of humble persons;*
> *First by the fathers' will and the counsel*
> *of friends,*
> *And then by their own mutual assent,*
> *as the two might agree.*

William Langland lived in a sophisticated age. He knew the difference between counsel and assent. The bride and bride-groom-to-be gave the latter; the friends tendered the former. To Lang-

---

1 *Piers Plowman*, B text, Passus IX, lines 113–115; G. C. Homans, *English Villagers in the Thirteenth Century* (Cambridge, Mass., 1942), p. 160.

land, the distinction was familiar and clear. Perhaps it had not
always been so; but at all times the ingredient of counsel, at
least, was part of the fabric of medieval life.

Counsel was as familiar among the nobility as among the peasants. We get an incidental glimpse of it when an Anglo-Norman
knight at the time of the Angevins asked for the counsel of his
followers in a moment of crisis:

> Roger d'Estutevile addresses his trusted friends
> And says: Barons, knights, say what you advise.

In such matters, the lord patterned his life on that of the king,
and when the institution of a small council was evolved, it was
used by the magnates as well as by the ruler. Listening to counsel
in the baronial hall was part of a noble's way of life.[2]

The king himself was, of course, more than a feudal lord, and
the tradition of counsel was, in his case, a little more complex.
The monarch was not only the supreme lord, he was also the *rex*,
anointed of the Lord God; he ruled over the subjects and was
alone in his dignity. The essence of his duty, as St. Isidore of
Seville pointed out in the seventh century, was to rule. The Emperor Charles III of Germany spoke in this tradition in 887 when
he declared that it behooved the Imperial dignity to exercise the
care of all subjects. This emphasis on power gave little place for
the need of counsel, and it found some support in both the teachings of the Church about political authority and in the eleventh
century revival of Roman Law; though there were conflicting
elements in each system of thought. St. Paul had given to the
church the injunction: "Be ye subject to every ordinance of
man for the Lord's sake"; whilst Roman Law gave to the lawyers
Quod principi placuit legis habet vigorem (what pleases the prince
has the force of the law). Both Roman and ecclesiastical traditions were strong on authority and somewhat weak on counsel.
Nevertheless, they envisaged a king who ruled in harmony with
his subjects, not one who scorned their cooperation and advice.
In any case, as suggested above, feudal kings and lords lived
essentially by feudal custom and tradition; and both envisaged
a monarch sitting upon his throne surrounded by his faithful

2 Feudal counsel is well analyzed in a brief passage by Professor Langmuir,
Document 2.

vassals, who did not regard his power as being absolute and who owed him the duty of both feudal aid when he required it and feudal counsel when he asked for it (and sometimes when he did not). Feudal kings could not hope to rule effectively without counsel and cooperation by the great lords; the monarchy simply did not possess the machinery and organization for authoritarian rule. And the only practical way to make the necessary contact with the magnates of the realm was to summon them to some general assembly in which communication could be by word of mouth.

Of course, there is a serious problem, involving differences of opinion, as to what such communication implied. Did the king seek a collective opinion or did he only consult individuals? How far did an individual's counsel bind him morally to support any action taken in agreement with it? On the other hand, how far was the king, if he summoned a general assembly, free to disregard completely the advice he received? Professor Fawtier believed that in the assemblies of France the king did not seek a genuine consent from his vassals. Even the counsel he sought was at best perfunctory. The ruler wanted acclamation for proposals. He wanted to make sure of a favourable public opinion for contemplated action, but he did not think of seeking a formal agreement and he did not contemplate disagreement. There was no real question of the community of subjects giving or withholding agreement to something which the ruler proposed.[3] But Professor Fawtier may have been thinking particularly of the earlier assemblies, not those of the twelfth and thirteenth centuries. These have more recently been carefully examined by Professor Langmuir, whose work is illustrated by an extract below.[4] It has taken us a significant step forward in our understanding of the distinction between counsel and consent in the general assemblies of France.

The earlier assemblies elsewhere closely resembled those described by Professor Fawtier. Those of Spain, Professor Marongiu believes, fell clearly in the same category: "The participants did not discuss or propose: they merely acclaimed, giving solemnity and publicity to some expression of the sovereign's will." Simi-

3 Document 3.
4 Document 2.

larly, he observes, the Icelandic assembly of Thingvellir, which has been described as the most ancient legislative assembly of Europe, was a typical example of this kind of meeting: the members assembled in the open plain, listened to the proposals of the wise man Ulfljøt, and acclaimed them.[5]

There may have been less acclamation and more serious discussion in the early Anglo-Saxon Witan; but nevertheless what the king wanted was essentially individual advice, even though it has been suggested that as early as the sixth century king Eathelbert of Kent used a "council," and that with a draft of the "legislation" before it, the council discussed, suggested amendments, and made additions,[6] just like a most up-to-date body of today. It is likely that we must banish from our minds such a sophisticated procedure and think rather of a loose and undefined body of advisers with whom a king discussed his problems, and who gave him individual counsel, each man expressing his own opinion and the king then making up his mind. That is how Edwin of Northumbria acted when he made a momentous decision to accept Christianity in 627. He was described as asking his counsellors "each one in turn how this doctrine, hitherto unknown, and this new worship of God seemed to him."[7] King Aethelstan in the tenth century still looked to his Witan for counsel, probably individual counsel, "I have consulted with my Witan," he said, "and I have found that they are heartily willing to go where I will." He had obviously been anxious to sound out the feelings of his magnates, but it is unlikely that he had sought a collective agreement to his plans.

It seems likely that we have to reject a recent suggestion[8] that the Anglo-Saxon kings could legislate only with the consent of the Witan, though of coure, it was asking for trouble to make a law if every member of the Witan who was asked advised against it. The situation on the eve of the Norman Conquest has been

5 Antonio Marongiu, *Il Parlamento in Italia*, trans. and adapted by S. J. Woolf, *Medieval Parliaments, A Comparative Study* (London, 1968), p. 66.

6 H. G. Richardson and G. O. Sayles, *Law and Legislation from Aethelbert to Magna Carta* (Edinburgh, 1966), pp. 11–12.

7 *Ecclesiastical History*, edited by Charles Plummer, vol. I, pp. 111–12. Notice the individual reply to a question which was directed to each in turn.

8 H. G. Richardson and G. O. Sayles, as above, p. 35.

stated eloquently by Professor Oleson, in words quoted below;[9] and we know that the feudal *Curia Regis* of William the Conqueror (1066–1087) continued many of the traditions of the Witan. Hence, we may venture to apply to William's "legislation" the words of the French lawyer Beaumanoir, even though these were written in the thirteenth century:[10]

"Etablissements must be made, except in crises of war or invasion, for sufficient cause, for the common profit, not against God and good customs, and by great counsel (*par grant conseil*)."

Nothing is said of the need for agreement or consent.

In any case, even if collective agreement had been desired in the time of William the Conqueror, it would have been almost impossible to obtain effectively. In the highly individualistic feudal society of that day, every great lord was bound to the king by a personal bond, and each had his own rights and liberties. The chronicler Matthew Paris was to comment on the individualism of the English feudal lords as late as the thirteenth century.[11] Agreement, except man to man, presupposed a sense of common interests on the part of the barons, and a capacity for common action, both lacking in the Conqueror's time.

The procedure by counsel rather than by agreement was hard to break. It had dominated political action for many centuries and was thoroughly congenial. It was natural in a primitive society in which contacts between the king and his great men were largely social and usually informal. The king rarely made great demands, but he gave the lords leadership and support. The lords had no heavy obligations, except in war, but they recognized the ruler as the king pin (if a pun may be permitted) of the social and political order. Common interests coupled with limited demands made it easy to arrive on most occasions at a consensus without the need for formal procedures, as is common in University committees and Senates, almost by a process of osmosis. This picture of the general assembly of magnates may

9 Document 1.

10 *Coutûmes de Beauvaisis*, edited by A. Salmon (Paris, 1900) Vol. II, p. 264.

11 See the description of the magnates going home from the general assembly of 1255, each to take is own counsel "in the manner of Englishmen," quoted Chapter III, Document XII.

be somewhat idyllic, but at least we can see how informality and individual contacts usually served the purpose of consultation between the king and his magnates in the early feudal state.

What we shall examine in the following pages is a tranformation of government and politics that made this procedure inadequate to preserve the old feudal tradition of co-operation between the king and the lords. The change is bound up with the emergence of what is known as the territorial state that was larger and more centralized than the feudal kingdom. One of its most striking features was normally a great increase in the power of the ruler, now armed with a more efficient instrument of rule, devoted professional servants, more wealth, and the means to raise armies from mercenaries and other sources as well as from his tenants-in-chief. This made ever more urgent the question of the relations between the monarch and the great magnates, and created a need for developing a new sophistication and definition, even a new regularity, in the old feudal assembly. There was an awareness on the part of the magnates that the form of cooperation which had served their forefathers well was no longer effective. On the other hand, kings increasingly recognized that they could bind magnates more effectively to a common enterprise, if they substituted collective agreement for individual advice. The issues were not nearly as clear to contemporaries as they may seem to us with the hindsight of history and greater political experience; but there seems to be little doubt that their emergence was one cause of a political revolution that began obscurely in the eleventh and twelfth centuries, and which transformed the feudal assembly and with it the practice of politics during the remarkable age of Simon de Montfort in England, Frederick II in Italy, and king Peter III of Aragon in Spain.

1 *A Canadian Scholar on Counsel in the Anglo-Saxon Witan*

In a very real sense, then, there is no such thing as a witenagemot, there are only witan [wise men]. There is no council, there is only counsel. There is not a shred of evidence to show that the witan ever regarded themselves as a corporate assembly, having an independent, if derivative, existence apart from the king. The wita is one whom the king consults, the witenagemot the occasion on which consultation takes place, or the act of consultation or deliberation. Nor is this strange. Certain things, for example the attestation of land charters, or the deeming of dooms, are done by the king with the counsel of the witan. One may, if one wishes, call the occasion a council. But to an Anglo-Saxon the distinction between council and counsel would have been meaningless. In fact, he would only recognize counsel. In his view the king would receive counsel, only in that sense does he hold a witenagemot. That this witenagemot was a body possessing certain powers or functions, or having even a vaguely defined constitution, is impossible. It is true that certain men customarily attended the king and were in a sense the natural counsellors of the king, but they offered counsel as individuals and not as members of a definite body or council possessed of certain powers and having a more or less fixed membership. It is true that they were considered representatives of the people, but an individual is as representative of the people as a hundred individuals. In a society in which law is sovereign this must needs be so.

SOURCE. Tryggvi J. Oleson, *The Witenagemot in the Reign of Edward the Confessor* (Toronto, 1955), p. 62. Reprinted by permission of the University of Toronto Press, Toronto, Canada.

2   An American Historian on Counsel and Agreement in the General Assemblies of France

... For Bloch, like Carlyle and Kern, has stressed that, "According to the code of government then universally acknowledged, no chief, whoever he might be, could decide anything important without having taken counsel."

That obligation to give and take counsel was an old obligation with deep roots. The obligation to give counsel existed before the creation of feudal law and later became incorporated into feudalism as one of the two positive duties of the vassal. The obligation to take counsel is already explicitly enunciated in the statements of Lothaire of France, Abbo of Fleuri, and Hugh Capet to the effect that a king could not and should not rule without the counsel of his magnates. It is still very much alive two centuries later, as can be seen in Rigord's description of Philip Augustus as accustomed always to use the counsel and wisdom of the archbishops, bishops, and greater princes of the kingdom in his frequent affairs requiring deliberation—and we might note that Rigord does not speak of the advice of the *curia*. The enduring importance of the obligation to give and take counsel is undeniable, but the reason for its importance is less evident.

Why does counsel confront us in canon law, in charter after charter, and on page after page of the chronicles, in connection with a multitude of decisions in all areas of life from the convent to the battlefield? Although there is only too abundant evidence of the use of counsel, *consilium* has never received the attention that has been paid to its companion term *auxilium* (aid). The historians of political theory have discussed it, but because of their concern with the medieval conception of law and lawmaking, they limited their examination of counsel to that con-

SOURCE. By Gavin Langmuir, in "Counsel and Capetian Assemblies," in *Studies Presented to the International Commission for the History of Representative and Parliamentary Institutions*, vol. 18 (1958), pp. 26–28. Reprinted by permission of the Publications Universitaires de Louvain, Belgium. Professor Langmuir's distinction between counsel and consent has been questioned by R. S. Hoyt in *A. H. R.*, Vol. 55 (July, 1960), p. 867.

text and, by a thorough confusion of counsel and consent, described counsel as a peculiar kind of community ratification or assent. . . . A superior might seek counsel to ensure the wisdom of any kind of decision, but he had to seek consent only when the execution of a decision would infringe the rights of others in order to make the decision legally applicable to them. When the king took counsel on a decision that did not affect the rights of others but fell clearly within his acknowledged rights, it was the king who, through consultation, decided what he should do; it was his exercise of his rights in commanding the necessary actions which gave his decision legal force. No consent was necessary. Any attempt to understand royal consultation should, therefore, differentiate between the very many occasions on which he also sought consent. For governing, in all its aspects, was far more than the definition or application of law; many decisions were severely practical and only related to existing rights most indirectly. For such decisions the king did not need consent, but on many of them he took counsel. . . .

[p. 33] Yet once the monarchy had gained outstanding power and stature by these traditional means, the ancient royal obligation to consult became highly susceptible to modification. . . . During the thirteenth century, the development of professional jurists and bureaucrats and the impact of effective royal power, internal peace, and the personality of St. Louis, made the monarchy seem ever more clearly the chief representative of the whole community and the principal source of wisdom and morality. The importance attached to baronial counsel declined correspondingly. Yet the fourteenth century was to show that, although the old belief in the wisdom and morality of the community was declining, it was by no means dead.

[English]

3   Counsel in the French General Assemblies, According to French Historians

In regard to . . . Capetian assemblies, these meetings of the enlarged Court of the king, we have made practically no progress since the days long ago when Achille Luchaire worked upon them. We may thus repeat the conclusions which this historian arrived at in 1891.[1]

"Looking at the matter closely, once the Assembly had gathered, it possessed neither a right to initiate nor a right to a regular vote. However great the number of those present, never more than a very few of the great men were called on to deliberate. The others, the multitude, those of a moderate or low status, could do no more than give expression to their agreement by their acclamation. Moreover, this restricted deliberation does not seem to have possessed any quality of independence. The great men ratify the royal will. They sanction the accomplished act or the decision taken by the immediate entourage of the king. They do not put forward their own proposals (leur propre résolution), still less can they make them prevail. The king consults, requires agreement, but the definitive resolution always depends on him alone. This fact is undeniable even for the XIth century, the golden age of feudal independence and power. We have seen King Robert consult his great lords, on a project dear to his heart. He wished to cause his son to be crowned, and he discounted completely the disapproval of his advisers. This is perhaps the sole example to be found in the history of the Capetian assemblies of a proposal arising from the royal initiative which did not gain agreement. When the king had a fear that he would not obtain approval he refrained from seeking advice from the feudal lords and only sought that of his curiales. Towards the end of the XIIth century a pacific revolution was achieved; it resulted in the end in depriving the lords of a knowledge not only of trials but

SOURCE. Ferdinand Lot and Robert Fawtier, Histoire des Institutions Françaises au Moyen Age, Vol. II (Paris, 1958), p. 547. Translated by permission of the Presses Universitaires de France, Paris, France.

[1] Histoire des Institutions monarchiques de la France sous les Premiers Capétiens (987–1180), second edition, ed. by A. Picard (Paris, 1891).

of the greater part of all administrative and political affairs. All real power lay in the hands of the members of the royal household (*Palatins*). The assembly of the magnates did no more than register the decisions of the small council and strengthen them with a sanction which, strictly speaking, was not even indispensable."

These Capetian assemblies performed a role which amounted to no more than approval; but they none the less stood for the possibility of control even if this did not exist. They kept alive the tradition of counsel offered to the ruler by the assembly of his vassals, in an enlarged council which comprised more than the king's Household alone.

Assemblies of this kind were possible only whilst the royal power was extended over a very limited area. But the day came when the royal domain in effect expanded to include all the realm or, to put it more precisely, distributed itself throughout all the realm. Then, questions of a practical kind began to present themselves. The Council was enlarged to the dimensions of an assembly,—of a parliament (*Parlement*) as they then said. It is easy to imagine (and it is not necessary to exaggerate) that a king residing in Paris should consult directly with a certain number of his vassals in the Ile-de-France, or even with them all. It may equally be imagined that the king who perambulated might make direct contact with his vassals in various parts of his domain which were farther away from Paris. But what is beyond imagination is that the king might summon a Parliament of his vassals throughout all his realm. Yet in this way alone could there have been some show of an element of control. . . .

The only control which, for a long period, could be exercised over royal acts was by the royal power itself. If the king only undertook operations which he was able to sustain by himself, without having to appeal for an extraordinary aid from all his subjects, there was no means of preventing him. His Council, that is to say his immediate entourage could advise against a proposed action, but the king was always at liberty to reject this advice. If the king had need to ask for either a financial or a military aid from his great barons, it was necessary to have an understanding with them; but even then it was not necessary to consult them in a body. It was enough to carry on a series of separate negotiations, which was always easier to do. . . .

Thus, the organization of the French kingdom did not anticipate any control over the monarch. For if it was understood that the king should consult his Council, it was equally understood that it was the king and not the Council that made the decision. Once the royal decision was made the Council had no other course but to bow to it. It is understandable that under these conditions there was no control whatever, and no opposition, in regard to the royal decisions, up to the time when the extraordinary growth of the domain, which was a feature of the reigns of Philip III the Bold (1270–1285) and Philip the Fair (1285–1314) would place at the disposal of the king an extent of land much greater than that which had been envisaged by those who, more or less consciously, had organized the Capetian monarchy,

[French]

CHAPTER II

THE TRANSITION FROM FEUDAL COUNSEL TO PARLIAMENTARY CONSENT

The growth of government in the eleventh and twelfth centuries caused progress in many aspects of life; but it brought its own problems and difficulties. It created a state held together not so much by the old feudal loyalties as by the royal power and a sense of the obligation of all men to the common well-being. The king increased both his authority and his majesty, but he was removed from the old familiar contact with his subjects. He rendered much greater service to those over whom he ruled; but he was compelled to ask more in return. Being human, some kings tended to abuse their growing power. The greatest threat to the harmony of the kingdoms was not now the weakness of the ruler, but the danger that he was becoming too strong. The greatest problem was that of curbing the actions of kings, not that of suppressing overmighty feudal lords.

The feudal assembly had been adequate for earlier needs, but it became quite inadequate for dealing with the problems of a complex government. As a result, the old harmonies declined; but if these were lost in the general session of the *Curia* it is hard to see where they could be rediscovered in the multiplying organs of government, all of which tended to reflect only the authority of the king. On the other hand, the increasing sophistication of kings and magnates, and the growth of the new institutions, created a deeper understanding of political problems and an unprecedented capacity for dealing with them. In particular, these changes tended to transform the general assembly. They marked it off from other sessions of the *Curia* and helped to give it distinctive functions of its own. Thus, it may be said that with the evolution of the territorial state, the problem of co-operation between the king and the magnates achieved a new dimension; and that materials now existed for solution such as had not been possible before.

All the countries of Europe had the same problem, in some cases with special complications. France had her regionalism, Germany had both regionalism and a special relationship to the Imperial tradition of Charlemagne, and Spain had her crusading kings. England was fortunate in spite of her militant aristocracy. Her traditions of cooperation between the central government and the local communities were strong. Neither in England nor anywhere else would it be easy to solve the political problem created by the territorial state; but the materials existed, especially in England, for a remarkable attempt.

To understand the background for this, it is necessary to bear in mind a few facts about the rulers of Europe, and the development of their machines of government. With regard to the rulers only one or two names can be mentioned. Most of them were very successful. They ruled in a period when Europe was beginning to prosper and expand, as shown by the Norman Conquest of Sicily from Islam, the Christian Reconquest in Spain against the Moors, and the First Crusade of 1096. Germany was the most brilliant and influential state in the eleventh century, home of the Holy Roman Empire (though, as we all learn in school, this was neither holy, nor Roman, nor even an Empire, in spite of the fact that it carried on some of the imperial notions of Rome). Its history was dominated throughout by the attempt of the Emperors to develop their powers in Germany, and later in Italy, and by the struggle of Empire and Papacy which lasted intermittently from 1076 to the death of the Emperor Frederick II in 1250 and beyond. During this long period there were many brilliant Emperors, but the only one to have an outstanding connexion with the beginnings of parliament was Frederick II, whose character is commented on below.

France, during the eleventh and twelfth centuries was culturally strong but politically weak. It was beset by internal divisions, the most important being that between the South and the North, between Languedoc and Languedöil, a cleavage the importance of which was almost unimpaired until the Albigensian Crusade by the Northerners in 1208–9. The spirit of its rulers is artistically, if not quite accurately, reflected in the well-known words of

King Louis VII, addressed to the Anglo-Norman courtier and scholar Walter Map, in 1179:

"Few men can have everything. The kings of the Indies are rich in precious stones and rare beasts: the Emperor of Byzantium and the King of Sicily are rich in gold and silks, though their men are useless in war and good only for talk; the German Emperor has no gold or silk or other luxuries, but he is rich in warlike men and horses; your lord, the King of England, has everything: men, horses, gold, silk, gems, wild beasts—everything. We in France have nothing. Only bread and wine and joy."

Of course, this was said, somewhat ironically, towards the end of Louis' only moderately successful reign, at a time when the Norman ruler of England had more land in France than the French king himself. French kings, as we shall see, had to make do with "bread and wine and joy" until the reign of Philip Augustus (1180–1223), referred to briefly below.

The English king to whom Louis VII referred was Henry II, who ruled over what has been called the Angevin "Empire," including England, Normandy and Aquitaine. This made him and his successors great European monarchs, although king John (1199–1216) lost possession of Normandy in 1204. Despite Louis VII's denigration of his own estate, Germany, France and England were the greatest centres of political power in Europe in the twelfth and thirteenth centuries.

It is perhaps worth mentioning a few outstanding rulers, particularly in the thirteenth century, the period when monarchies were most intimately connected with parliamentary growth.

If we have to choose one individual, from a long line of famous German Emperors, this must be Frederick II, who died in 1250. At the time of his death, he was the most brilliant ruler in the West, called by his contemporaries Wonder of the World. His title was well earned by his intellectual gifts, his questioning outlook, and his political skill. He not only ruled Germany, but also acquired the kingdom of Sicily through his mother Constance, heiress to the Norman rulers. He was familiar with Arab, German, and Italian culture. He had been born at Jesi in Ancona on 26 December, 1194, in a tent around which were gathered fifteen cardinals and bishops safeguarding the integrity of the royal birth; and he had spent his youth in the Arab and Norman part of his lands. He was by far the most cultured and widely experienced ruler of his age.

Hardly less influential was the French ruler St. Louis who built on the foundations laid by Philip Augustus, and who added a remarkable contribution of his own. He was king from 1226–1270, and he created a royal image unique in his day and perhaps in all the annals of medieval Europe, composed of chivalry, love of justice, and Christian devotion and humility. He led two unsuccessful Crusades, one in 1248 and the other in 1270; during the latter he died. His arbitration was much sought after in the quarrels of Europe, and he gave a famous judgement on the dispute between Henry III of England and his barons that is referred to below.

Both St. Louis and Frederick II encouraged a tendency towards absolute power in rulers, though in very different ways; Frederick's attitude was secular and cynical, while Louis' was deeply religious, though he was no slave to his priests. Both contributed to the majesty of kings; but the influence of St. Louis was the more enduring. Frederick's power collapsed with his death and never completely recovered; Louis' memory was cherished by Frenchmen for generations and coloured their whole concept of the monarchy. His nobility of character was more dangerous to the political liberty of his subjects than all the pragmatism and cynicism of the Emperor.

In the century of Frederick II and St. Louis, England could not boast of any ruler quite as outstanding; but nevertheless she had three striking kings, each of whom made a contribution to the royal tradition and to the development of parliament. Two of them, at least, were very able men. King John was formidable and unscrupulous; it was fortunate for England that he could not win the loyalty of the barons or prosper in his wars. (As every schoolboy knows, king Richard Coeur de Lion (1189–99) had benefited the kingdom by his absence, John now did the same by his follies and crimes.) King Henry III (1216–1272) inherited a monarchy weakened by the loss of Normandy and by the revolt against John; and it was weakened further by his own minority. He was tenacious of his royal power and had some of the instincts of an autocrat; here again England was fortunate that a monarch who ruled for fifty-six years was neither too weak nor too strong. Of this colourful and in some ways attractive ruler it has been written:[1]

"In truth his abilities were incommensurate with his ambitions; he was for ever trying more than he could achieve. He stooped to tricks and evasions, and more than once, by his failure to understand the changing world around him, built up an opposition as unanimous and formidable as that of his father's reign. Dante placed him in a region of purgatory reserved for simpletons; but his 'simplicity' was, it has been said, a kind of innocence which remained in him all his life and gave him an appeal to both contemporaries and posterity even when he was at his worst."

Edward I (1272–1307) was the greatest English parliamentarian of the thirteenth century; but he wanted parliament on his own terms. He was quicker to appeal for the patriotic support of his subjects, in his well-intentioned wars and reforms, than he was in taking them into a true partnership. But by the time his reign began, the foundations of the English parliamentary assembly had been well and truly laid; his paternalism did little more than contribute to its future growth already ensured by the events of the great age of Simon de Montfort discussed in some detail below.

In Spain, there was an abundance of able and successful kings, (some of whom will be mentioned in a moment); but the most important feature of the period to be borne in mind is the great war of liberation from the Moors in which almost every single monarch of the various small Christian kingdoms was involved. The most important of these kingdoms was Castile which at the beginning of the twelfth century stretched from the Bay of Biscay to include Toledo on the river Tagus. Next to Castile on the West was the smaller kingdom of León which united with its larger neighbour in 1230, an event which gave a tremendous impetus to the Christian attack. The kingdom of Aragon in the Northeast was similarly formed by the union of two neighbours, and expanded not only southwards but also eastwards into the islands of the Mediterranean. In between León-Castile and Aragon in the far north, the small kingdom of Navarre had no opportunity to expand.

---

[1] B. Wilkinson, *The Later Middle Ages in England* (London, 1969), p. 54.

The great days of the liberation fell between 1034 and 1248. In the first of these years, the Christians captured the Caliphate of Cordova; in the second, Seville was taken by Ferdinand III king of Castile. Thus many rulers before the thirteenth century contributed to the dominant traditions of Spain: Ferdinand I who died at León in 1065, "having smitten the Muslim power on all his frontiers, which he extended in all directions;" Alfonso I of Aragon, called the Warrior, who died in 1134; Alfonso VII of Castile who bore the proud title of Emperor when he was crowned at León in 1135; and a successor in the same kingdom, Alfonso VIII, who achieved a brilliant victory at Las Navas de Tolosa in 1212. The Spanish kingdoms were not isolated from the rest of Christendom in their struggle. They received help from knights of many countries, especially Normans and Frenchmen. As a Castilian king remarked, when asked to cooperate in a Crusade to the East, "We are always on crusade here, and so we do our share." The two monarchs mentioned below, Alfonso I of León and Peter III of Aragon, were typical products of their age. They created the image of a king who was above all a successful warrior, and who summoned the Cortes when he had a special need of support for his wars.

We know much more about the kings than about the Spanish magnates. Typical of the Spanish hero was Ruy Diaz de Vivar, the Cid, one of the greatest warriors and legendary heroes of the Middle Ages, who died in 1099. He had no interest in attempting to modify the form of government of any Spanish kingdom, only in waging successful war. Very different was the French-English leader of the barons against Henry III, Simon de Montfort. It is true that he was active a century and a half after the Cid; but the difference between the two is striking. Simon helped to produce a great constitutional document incorporating the concept of parliament, and died defending his interpretation of it.[2] The atmosphere in which he and his fellow magnates worked may be illustrated by the words of Sir Maurice Powicke:[3]

"A man of his kind is not inspired by lofty conceptions of law so

---

[2] Document 3.

[3] *King Henry III and the Lord Edward* (Oxford, 1947), p. 391. The passage is printed with some comments in my *Constitutional History of Medieval England, 1216–1399*, Vol. I (London, 1948), pp. 150–151.

much as by the exaltation of a crusader. The best devices could be overthrown by that 'mischance' which dogs the heroes of romances. [then follows a quotation from a contemporary of Simon, describing the efforts of the reformers] 'The barons have much to do. They go to work fiercely. God grant that they succeed. Many heads, many opinions. Novelty breeds discord.' "And when vision faded and mischance came, Sir Maurice remarks, Simon went on as a dark force.

Similar men and moods no doubt lurked beneath the surface at the great moments of creation in other countries, but they cannot now be recaptured. Nevertheless, we may assume their existence as we glance at one or two efforts to devise parliamentary assemblies in the course of the thirteenth century, and in France as late as 1302. The magnates no doubt, as Professor Myers says,[4] may have attended the general assemblies summoned by their kings primarily to defend their privileges; but some of them, at least, may have attended also from a sense of obligation to their ruler and to the community of their district, and even to the kingdom itself.

With regard to the development of the machine of government, it is necessary to be more specific, for without some understanding of this, the conditions which made the creation of parliaments possible cannot be understood. The purpose of the description which follows is to show how the early and rudimentary machine, subject to the king's personal control, became large and complicated, much of it far removed from personal contact with the ruler, and how this process affected the problem of government. England provides the obvious example. There, as elsewhere, for many centuries the kingdom was governed mainly through members of the king's household who constantly journeyed around the countryside, accepting hospitality from monasteries and great magnates, and carrying everything they needed on the backs of horses or in carts. But the machine of government slowly developed. As early as the seventh century, Anglo-saxon kings issued solemn charters or dipomas in which they recorded grants to their subjects. King Alfred (871–899) may have issued orders in a more businesslike writ, economical of parchment and words and authenticated with a seal. King Edward the Confessor (1042–1066)

4 Introduction, Document 2.

had a seal which bore on both sides a portrait of the king enthroned in majesty. It was three inches across and was derived through King Cnut (1016–1035) from the seal of the German Emperor. The first royal secretary whose name has come down to us served king Alfred's father Aethewulf: his name was Felix. Important offices developed in the royal household, such as that of Steward, Chamberlain, and Butler, perhaps referred to as early as *Beowulf* in the eighth century. A chronicler records that king Edmund was killed in 946 while defending his Steward in the royal Hall.

Through such developments, the political unity of England had been greatly advanced by 1066. In 1086, for example, William the Conqueror was able to obtain an oath of loyalty at Salisbury from every substantial landowner in England, whosesoever men they were; and as we shall see, this unity later had a profound influence on the growth of parliament. At the same time, the machine of government developed; and the process of expansion was accompanied by specialization of function and by differentiation between the various "departments" which is the hall-mark of a developing bureaucracy. The king's chancery, for example, beginning with clerks of his chapel, became a great secretariat in charge of the royal seal, and proceeded to acquire also important functions in administration and law. The treasury kept the king's moneys, and connected with it there grew up a powerful accounting office known as the exchequer. It, too, acquired extra duties.

Similarly, what we may call "departments" of the *Curia* emerged as great courts of Common Law which came to be known as the Court of King's Bench and the Court of Common Pleas. They heard some cases which had formerly come before the king in the undifferentiated *Curia Regis*, and they added many new ones in the course of the thirteenth century. All these "departments" in time, to use a phrase familiar to historians, "went out of court." Hence, they drifted further and further away from those solemn sessions of his court to which the king summoned the general body of his greater lords.

But even more significant was the emergence of still another "department," if such it may be called—a small group of the king's advisers who concentrated on giving counsel to the monarch, and who gradually became a clearly marked group of experts. One day this group would become the king's Privy Council.

Its members were an inner circle within the *Curia Regis*, distinct both from other "departments" and from the general assembly; and it is easy to see how the growth of their special duties diminished the king's tendency to look for counsel from the magnates in the larger assembly. This would cause some searching of heart on the part of the latter as to what their duties now were, or perhaps what they ought to be. The whole process of differentiation and specialization clearly had important consequences for the process of government at the very highest level.

There is not much difference of opinion about this general development, or about that of France, to be described in a moment; but there are very great differences in the interpretation of it, relative to the creation of parliament. One opinion, favoured below, is that when parliament emerged it would be heir to the general assembly of magnates. Another,[5] is that the parliamentary assembly was in essence a session of the king's council with the primary function of giving justice. The second one is hard to reconcile with the early process of differentiation and specialization, and in particular, with the origin and attributes of the "privy" council which have been suggested above.

The development of the small council can be seen as early as the reign of Henry II. Thomas Becket referred to the "familiars" by whose counsels the king acted. Henry II was noted as retiring with the same "familiars" into an inner room. He was described as listening patiently to what was said in open council and then revealing his mind secretly to those in whom he had the greatest trust. He sent commands to his earls and barons after taking counsel from his familiars. Henry III's council had clearly emerged by 1233; its members could claim that both king and kingdom were ruled by their counsel. In 1236, we read of a "chief councillor"; he and eleven others swore that they would give faithful counsel to the king.

The emergence of this small council made access by the magnates to the king more difficult unless they happened to be among those who were the king's familiars. It also underlined the need to put a curb upon the ruler whose power was beginning to overshadow the land and was not likely to be restrained by his intimate advisers. A good bureaucrat like Richard Fitzneal, treasurer

5 Chapter III, Document 11.

of Henry II, could justify unquestioning obedience to royal commands by the pious observation that all power was of God and
so must be obeyed.[6] In contrast, it was a little old-fashioned to
argue, as did the author of a tract called *What should be the
Office of a King?* (early thirteenth century) that the king ought
to do right in all things by the judgement of the magnates and by
their counsel. What was needed was something more; it was an
insistence that some commands, at least, were to be obeyed not
because all power came from God, but because they arose from
decisions agreed to by the lords.[7]

It is probable that the same general development was occurring
in France, though the evidence is more scanty. There was a similar process of disintegration and specialization in the *Curia*. For
many years the French king had his moneys kept by the knights
of the Temple; but by the middle of the reign of St. Louis he had
developed the financial activites of the *Curia*; and by 1309, under
the title of *Chambre des Comptes*, it rivalled the English exchequer. Gradually the magnates were excluded, and the experts
took over. In 1300 the latter complained that the great lords
hindered their work; and in reply the king bade the ushers of
the court to shut the doors during all the morning against "prelates, barons, and others of our council who come into the chamber to talk and importune you about matters other than those
with which you are busied." The king's household developed its
own offices of finance, the *Chambre aux Deniers* and the *Argen-
terie*. Alongside these were the secretarial offices of chancery and
chamber. But there was nothing comparable with the English
courts of King's Bench and Common Pleas. There was, however,
a small council whose members at least from 1269 took an oath of
office which gave them the particular duty of advice.

The broad consequences of this growth were similar to those
we have seen in England. But there were some important differences. The French *Curia* was much more heavily burdened with
judicial work. But this did not cause it to become essentially a
court, as is often supposed to have happened in England. Rather
it caused a process of bifurcation by which the French assembly
ultimately split into two separate institutions, one of which was

---

6 Document 1.

7 Some comments on this little known tract are given in Document 2.

primarily political (after 1302 called the States-General), and the other was essentially judicial (emerging under St. Louis as the *Parlement*, called the *Cour de Parlement* in 1345). This is true even though there were more political activities and less giving of justice in the *parlement* than used to be supposed.[8]

The process of bifurcation in the French *Curia* adversely affected the attendance of the magnates, especially at the *Parlements*. The legal sessions involved difficult problems with which great lords were not well equipped to deal; while the administration of justice demanded frequent and prolonged meetings which they disliked and could not afford. Hence there developed a difference between the two sessions of the French *Curia*, not only in function but also in personnel.

But in point of fact, the king could not count on the attendance of "all" or nearly all the great lords; even for important political decisions and for legislation in that part of the *Curia* that was to become the States-General, although the attendance was better here. In an ordinance for the Jews issued in 1223 and again in 1230, it was insisted that the enactment be held by both those who had agreed to it at the time of making and those who had not. Beaumanoir, as we have seen, did not insist on the presence of the general body of magnates when laws were made, but only on "great counsel." It is even probable that the king's small council was taken on some important occasions to represent the general body. King Louis, especially after his return from his first Crusade, made enactments simply with the advice of his council. With the extension of the royal domain, it became impossible to consult the general gathering of magnates in regard to many important decisions. Louis could boast that there was now only one king in France; but the king often merely demanded that the great lords should apply the royal ordinances on their lands.

The result of all this was a great weakening of the French general assembly in both its aspects, judicial and political. It has been observed that, while England produced a single institution in which the king gave justice and the community gave consent, France was compelled by circumstances to produce two, neither of

8 T. N. Bisson, "Consultative Functions of the King's Parliaments (1250–1314)," *Speculum*, Vol. 44 (July, 1969), pp. 353–373.

which, in consequence, had the strength of the English institution. It must be insisted that the English parliament was strong, not because of the dominance of justice in it, but because of the dominance of politics; or perhaps, more correctly, because of the combination of both, so that the administration of justice never crowded out the discussion of politics. It was precisely because the English parliament was never essentially either an expanded session of the council, or a court set above other courts, that it had the time, strength, and attributes to deal adequately with the great problems of public life.

It seems to be quite wrong to suggest that the English *Curia* owed much to developments in France, particularly to the *parlement*. Indeed, the English habit of disposing of political business in general assemblies seems to have developed a good deal more rapidly than the French, though perhaps it was also better recorded. At first the contribution of the magnates took the form, in the main, of the traditional counsel; but in time the idea of giving agreement rather than merely advice began to predominate. When the Conqueror in 1085 made an important decision in his Christmas *Curia*, he only had "a very deep conference with his Witan concerning this land." Similarly, in a famous letter to Archbishop Anselm immediately after his coronation, Henry I only promised to commit himself and his realm to the counsel of Anselm and those who had the right to stand alongside the Archbishop. King Henry II still looked for counsel rather than agreement from his barons. He claimed that when anything arose that concerned greater affairs, counsel was taken and the barons came together to give support to his business. Ranulf Glanville, his justiciar, defined the law as being promulgated by the counsel of the magnates and the authority of the king; though under Stephen, Henry I's successor, it was stated on one occasion (reportedly) that a measure enacted without the common consent of the barons could be valid only for the king's lifetime.

But the practice of "treating," which led to agreement, gradually becomes more evident. King Henry II was familiar with it. In 1154 he summoned his chief men to "treat" about the state of the kingdom and the reformation of the peace, and again in the following year, this time concerning the conquest of Ireland. In connection with his famous Assize of Clarendon in 1166, he got the agreement of the magnates as well as their advice. Similarly, during a time of trouble in 1177, he again treated with them about the peace and stability of the realm.

In military affairs, the practice at this time has been described[9] as conforming in a general way to the principle that defensive wars and field strategy required no more than a prudent consultation. The undertaking of foreign expeditions and offensive wars necessitated a vassal-warriors' consent.

The magnates were also familiar with the idea of "treating." The fact that Henry I had not obtained their consent to the marriage of his daughter Matilda to Geoffrey of Anjou was said to have created a general belief that they were freed from their oath to accept Matilda as queen. Before the battle of Alnwick in the reign of Henry II, the barons of Yorkshire were said to have "treated" in common (*in commune*) about tactics; in the absence of their king it was not enough merely to give each other advice; they needed an agreed plan.

Another form of treating together became prominent towards the end of the twelfth century. This was described as acting "by common counsel"; but it was something more than the old-fashioned procedure by which the king received counsel from his lords. It was apparently action by a group in which there was communing together with a view to common action; what was wanted was a general agreement rather than a decision by a particular individual on the basis of the advice he received. Thus every member of the group would have a responsibility in any action that ensued. As early as 1100, King Henry I was described as having been crowned by the mercy of God and the common counsel of the barons. In 1190, England was to be ruled by common counsel in the absence of Richard Coeur de Lion on his Crusade; and Richard directed from Messina that the magnates should "treat" with his council in England in order to dispose of such business. As a result, it was agreed by common deliberation that there should be united action; and this was exemplified in a famous assembly at Lodden Bridge which met to treat about certain great and arduous business of the lord King and of the realm. As a consequence of these experiences, it is probable that the distinction between counsel and agreement was more and more

[9] T. N. Bisson, "Military Origins of Medieval Representation," *A.H.R.*, Vol. 71 (July, 1966), p. 1209.

clearly recognized. When, in Richard's reign, Walter of Coutances was raised by the magnates to be justiciar, he promised to do nothing in the government except by the will and consent of his associates, and by the counsel of the barons of the exchequer. Despite their high title, the barons of the exchequer were the king's professional servants, and their contribution to Walter's government was not to be agreement but only advice.

The consequences of these changes were apparent in the reign of King John. In 1205, John summoned his magnates together "to treat with us concerning our great and arduous business and the common profit of our realm." He later became a vassal of the Holy See "of our own free will and by the common counsel of the barons." In the Magna Carta it was laid down that taxation beyond the customary feudal aids should be by the counsel of all the tenants-in-chief. The exact words were, "the common counsel of our kingdom."[10] Behind the Magna Carta, it is now recognized, lay a change in political climate, a development in the attitude toward public affairs which was of outstanding significance.[11] It was this general change that tended to transform the assembly of magnates. The culmination of the development came in the thirteenth century; but it now seems clear that this was only the end of a long process which had filled at least the whole period of the Angevin kings.

Similar changes also occurred in France, though at a slower pace. For this, there were a good many reasons. One was the weakness of the French kings before Philip Augustus, combined with the limited extent of the royal domain. Closely connected was the well-known regionalism in France, which made French lords much more indifferent than the English to action in the general assembly. Nevertheless, French kings summoned this assembly from an early period, and they sometimes sought agreement in it as well as advice.[12]

In 1179, King Louis VII summoned barons and prelates from all his kingdom. He planned to associate his son Philip Augustus with him in the kingship, and he wanted their assent and not

[10] Document 5.

[11] H. G. Richardson and G. O. Sayles, *The Governance of Medieval England* (Edinburgh, 1963), pp. 368, 372.

[12] Chapter I, Document 2.

merely their advice. Similar cooperation was sought by his successor in 1185, when it was proposed to give aid in the Holy Land against the infidels. Again, in 1213, "all" the magnates were asked to assent to an invasion of England. The chroniclers frequently stated that all the great lords were summoned, and that all, or nearly all, were there. They came, a modern writer has said, "for deliberation, to treat, to give counsel," and it is difficult, with the scanty evidence which has survived, to distinguish one purpose from another; but Professor Langmuir believes that most of the matters discussed needed baronial cooperation, and a surprising number depended on baronial consent.

In spite of this, the French general assembly failed to achieve the vitality of the English, and this is partly to be explained by simple historic accident. Though the French kings were still comparatively restricted in their control over their kingdom, they were represented in the thirteenth century by very remarkable and successful rulers. Philip Augustus, who ruled at the beginning of it, was the hero of the recovery of Normandy from the English; while St. Louis, who died in 1270, was an outstanding and masterful personality whose achievements have been touched on above. Both Kings greatly strengthened the monarchy by far-reaching improvements in the machinery of government.

The French kings now symbolized a remarkable predominance of their country over all its neighbours in learning, culture, and chivalry. The cult of the monarch became part of the French political tradition. Moreover, the demands of the kings on their subjects remained limited despite the expansion of the domain. Thus there were many and varied reasons why the general assembly in France did not witness any spectacular change until the glories of the age of Philip Augustus and St. Louis had been left behind, and a new period of crisis came with the reign of Philip the Fair. Then we shall get the famous States-General of 1302.

The comparison between developments in England and France is illuminating. It shows how differences in geography and history could work to produce very dissimilar assemblies, even in countries which were intimately associated; and it also seems to show, incidentally, how far historians can be led astray by certain resemblances between the French *parlement* and other institutions; especially those English historians who are quite uncompromising in their view that the English parliament was in essence only the session of a court.

If we travel south from France into Spain, we find that the development of the general assembly was in some ways not only earlier but also more spectacular. Alfonso IX summoned an assembly in the kingdom of León as early as 1188, which contained "elected citizens" and to which he made remarkable concessions.[13] He granted that in the future he would not make treaties, war, or peace, except with the counsel of the bishops, nobles, and "good men," by whose counsel, he said, "I ought to rule." For their part, the bishops, knights, and members of the *curia* promised faithfully to counsel the king for the purposes of justice and peace. This has been regarded as creating a new political constitution for the country. It was, indeed, a very striking exchange of pledges. It might well have begun a new era. But the mutual promises had restrictions which should not be overlooked. In attempting to assess the significance of these, it seems imperative to bear fully in mind the close contacts referred to above between the various kingdoms of Europe; and to judge the development in León in the light of the distinction between counsel and "treaty" that had already appeared not only in León itself but also in England and France. If we do so, we shall have to conclude not, as has often been done, that the Spanish kingdom was in advance of other countries in the development of its general assembly, but rather that it was somewhat behind. At least, it seems that the king and his subjects were still preoccupied essentially with the problem of counsel in the general assembly. Nor was it apparently the "common counsel" of Richard I's reign in England, or of Magna Carta. As far as we can see, it was the old fashioned feudal counsel that, in however striking a setting, still dominated the lively assembly of León.

The difference between counsel and "treaty" is worth a further

13 Document 6. For conflicting interpretations, see Documents 7 and 8. Professor O'Callaghan has suggested, in *A.H.R.* Vol. 74 (June, 1969), p. 153, that the promise to be guided by the counsel of his subjects may not have been intended to set down a constitutional principle of permanent validity; and Evelyn S. Proctor has shown, in *E.H.R.* Vol. 85 (January, 1970) pp. 45–53, that in all probability Alfonso only promised to get the counsel of his *curia*, that is, of members of his court, on matters of war, peace, and treaties. This, she has suggested, was no more than a pledge to follow traditional procedures.

comment, for it is crucial to this study. It has been discussed by Professor Langmuir, who has been a pioneer in the delicate and difficult task of distinguishing, as far as possible, between medieval counsel and consent. He has rightly drawn attention to the need for agreement when the execution of a royal decision would involve the rights of others. But it may also be emphasized here that the political reason for seeking agreement was even more important. The king had to take into account, more and more, the expanding sense of the prelates and barons that they had a responsibility for the conduct of public affairs which could not be satisfied by the old-fashioned feudal consultation. They expected to give or withhold agreement; and this implied a new form of political cooperation as well as a defense of private rights. Thus, a new institution was gradually evolved, involving both legal and political obligations by the king and his subjects. The emergence of this in the course of the thirteenth century, to which the name "parliament" was often applied, will be discussed briefly in the next chapter below.

1   An American Historian Discusses the French and English Small Councils of the King

The same usage [as in France] is found in the English chronicles and records. In England, by 1237, this body [the council] was appointed and took an oath; the same is true in France at least from 1269 and probably much earlier. The institutionalization of the small royal council was part of the long trend towards specialization which had strengthened royal government. But the distinction between the sworn councillors and others was also symptomatic of the increasing breakdown of feudal sentiments and the sharper differentiation between the small group of gov-

SOURCE. Gavin Langmuir, "Politics and Parliaments in the Early Thirteenth Century," in Études sur l'Histoire des Assemblées d'États, Travaux et Recherches de la Faculté de Droit et des Sciences Économiques de Paris (Paris, 1966), p. 54. Reprinted by permission of the Publications Universitaires de Louvain, Louvain, Belgium.

ernmental specialists and the wider group of vassals, bound primarily by a legal obligation, who were summoned to royal assemblies for political reasons rather than for judicial and bureaucratic efficiency. This is the period in which magnates will complain that the king is not listening to the counsel of his natural counsellors.

[English]

2   *The* Dialogus de Scaccario *on the Duty* of *Obedience to the King in the Reign of the English King Henry II*

It is necessary to be subject to, in all fear, and similarly to obey, powers that are ordained by God. For all power is from the lord God. It does not therefore seem to be absurd or alien [to the nature of] ecclesiastics to preserve, by serving them, the rights of kings, as excelling all others, and also other powers; especially in those matters which are not opposed to truth and honesty. But one ought to serve them, not so much in maintaining the honours by which the glory of royal power is 'adorned, but rather [in maintaining] the abundance of their worldly resources which belong to them by reason of their status: it is these which make them illustrious, these which maintain them [in their power]. For the abundance of resources or lack of them either exalts or humbles the power of princes. Those who lack these resources will be a prey to their enemies; their enemies will fall as victims to those who possess enough. And although these resources may have frequently come to kings not by well-attested right but sometimes by ancestral laws, sometimes by the dark counsels of their own hearts, or occasionally by the arbitrement of their will alone, nevertheless their deeds are not to be discussed or condemned by their inferiors. For their hearts and the workings of their hearts

SOURCE. Translated from the *De Necessariis Observantiis Scaccarii Dialogus* ed. by A. Hughes, C. G. Crump and C. Johnson (Oxford, 1902) pp. 55–56, printed in Stubbs' *Select Charters* p. 200, with an important omission. By permission of the Clarendon Press, Oxford.

are in the hand of God, and the cause of those to whom the care
of subjects has been particularly entrusted by God Himself stands
or falls by Divine and not by human judgment. Nevertheless no-
body, however rich he may be, if he acts wrongly, deceives himself with impunity, for of such as he it is written "the powerful
shall suffer more powerfully the torments." Thus, whatever shall
be, or seem to be, the cause or manner of acquiring [such re-
sources] those who, by their office, have been deputed to their
custody should not be more remiss in their care. But there should
be diligent care in collecting preserving and distributing them,
as of reckoning the returns concerning the state of the realm,
through which it remains unharmed. We know, indeed, that by
prudence, by courage, by temperance and by justice and by other
virtues, powers and rights are preserved to the monarch; wherefore
to all the ministers of his land also they are to be insisted upon
with all our power.

[Latin]

3   *A Canadian Historian Discusses the Tract*
     "What Should Be the Office of a King?"
     Written at the Beginning of the
     Thirteenth Century

[The tract] illustrates the more general theory of the monarchy.
It is a compilation by an anonymous writer, possibly in the early
thirteenth century, which describes how the king should hold
his office. The writer appears to have been a moderately educated
layman with access to the records of London. He was a man with
strong political views which he promoted with evidence when he
could come by it and with forgery when he could not. He was
an imperialist with a "Whig" view of the monarch, whom he
wished to see strong but whom he wished also to see debarred

SOURCE. B. Wilkinson, *The Constitutional History of Medieval England
1216–1399*, Vol. III (London, 1958), pp. 84–85. Reprinted by permission of
the Longman Group, Harlow, England.

from the possibility of despotism such as John's by the need to act with the judgement of the magnates. He describes what ought to be, not what was; hence the fact that he believes the king ought to, or must, take an oath not to dismember the rights of the crown does not mean that the king took such an oath. Liebermann believed that the writer promoted a party programme; but it is not easy to distinguish any "party" to which he may have lent his support at any time in the early thirteenth century. He drew freely on the king's coronation promise and wanted his provision for just rule to be incorporated in a coronation oath.

Liebermann saw in the tract all those constitutional aims towards a parliamentary control over government which Stubbs reserved for the age of Edward I; and certainly the insistence on government with the counsel of the magnates is very striking. The king had to rule according to law. He had to do right by the judgement of the magnates of the realm, and to maintain justice with their counsel. Moreover, the writer anticipates thirteenth-century thought in his lively sense of the importance of the *regnum*. He even talks about the crown of the kingdom, using the same phrase which Edward I was to use in his letter to the pope in 1275, though how far he anticipated later ideas of an impersonal Crown it is impossible to say.

It is clear that the remarkable concepts of the writer need careful consideration, and that in any case his work must be regarded as showing an understanding of the urgent need to preserve the feudal limitations on the monarchy. At the same time, his writing gives an impression that the feudal limitations were in danger of becoming ineffective. The majesty of the ruler was casting its shadow over the liberties of the subject. The king, as in the Anonymous of York written between 1080 and 1104, was the Vicar of God. His office was the great hope of the subject for peace and justice. The people were his sons, under his protection. Despite Liebermann's suggestion, we are very far from the king who seeks the judgement of his people in parliament.

[English]

4   *Two English Historians Describe the Change*
of Political Climate Which Preceded
Magna Carta

The first question we should perhaps ask is why the barons'
struggle with John was political and not a mere contest for power
or political gain. To begin with, it may be well to say a little
of the barons themselves, for there seems to be some danger lest
they should come to be written off as unintelligent, self-seeking,
scoundrelly conspirators, so violent has been the reaction against
the idealisation of the very ordinary men who wrested the Great
Charter from an arbitrary and short-sighted king. Doubtless, since
they shared our common infirmities, they should have been better
men than they were; but no one, it might be thought, who had
read the Articles of the Barons and the Charter itself, could have
failed to recognize that behind these documents there lay a development in men's minds and in their attitude towards public
affairs that was of outstanding historical significance, a development to which no parallel can be found in any earlier century.
Even if the intrinsic merit of the articles and the charter be questioned, the fact that they are the first of their kind establishes in
itself their importance, for they are evidence that the barons who
devised them had become politically conscious. Here we have a
law, the foundation of our statute-book, imposed not from above,
as were Henry II's assizes, but from below, by those who, it is
true, would normally constitute an important element in the
king's council, but who, on this occasion, took the initiative.
Just as the Great Charter is the first of our statutes, so the
Articles of the Barons stand at the head of that long line of
formal statements of grievances which we can trace through the
Petition of the Barons of 1258 to the common petitions of Edward III's reign and which have given us the characteristic forms
of English legislation. . . . on however low a plane we place the
articles of the charter, whatever blunders and imperfections we
see in them and the men who made them, they demand a high

SOURCE. H. G. Richardson and G. O. Sayles, *The Governance of Medieval
England from the Conquest to Magna Carta* (Edinburgh, 1963), pp. 368–369.
Reprinted by permission of Edinburgh University Press, Edinburgh, Scotland.

place in our consideration as marking a stage in the political development of the country and the evolution of legislative forms. . . .

[English]

5   Clauses in Magna Carta Setting Forth a Right of Consent

12. Scutage or aid shall be levied in our kingdom only by the common counsel of our kingdom, except for ransoming our body, for knighting our eldest son, and for marrying our eldest daughter; and for these [purposes] only a reasonable aid shall be taken. The same provision shall hold with regard to aids of the city of London.

13. And the city of London shall have all its ancient liberties and free customs, both by land and water. Furthermore, we will and grant that all the other cities, boroughs, towns, and ports shall have all their liberties and free customs.

14. And in order to have the common counsel of the kingdom for assessing an aid other than in the three cases aforesaid, or for assessing a scutage, we will cause the archbishops, bishops, abbots, earls, and greater barons to be summoned individually by our letters; and we shall also cause to be summoned in general, through our sheriffs and bailiffs, all those who hold of us in chief . . . for a certain day, namely, at the end of forty days at least, and to a certain place. And in all such letters of summons we will state the cause of the summons; and when the summons has thus been made the business assigned for the day shall proceed according to the counsel of those who are present, even if all those summoned have not come.

[Latin]

SOURCE. Substantially as in J. C. Holt's *Magna Carta* (Cambridge, 1969), pp. 320–323. Reprinted by permission of Cambridge University Press, American Branch, New York, U.S.A. Professor Holt used the text in Bémont's *Chartes des libertés anglaises, 1100–1305* (Paris, 1892), pp. 26–30, collated with the original.

6   *Declaration by King Alfonso IX in the*
Cortes at León in 1188

The decree established by Alfonso King of León and Galicia
in the cortes at León, with the archbishop of Compostella and
with all the bishops and magnates of his kingdom and with
those chosen by the cities.

In the name of God. When I held a cortes at León with the
archbishop and the bishops and magnates of my kingdom, and
with the citizens chosen from every city, I Alfonso, King of León
and Galicia, established and confirmed with an oath that I would
preserve for all the inhabitants of my kingdom, whether clergy
or laity, the good customs which they enjoy, as established by my
predecessors.

I promised also that I would not make war or peace or treaties,
except with the counsel of the bishops, the nobles and the "good
men" by whose counsel I ought to rule.

[Latin]

SOURCE. *Cortes de los antiguous reinos de León y Castilla*, ed. by Manuel
Colmeiro, published by the Real Academia de la Historia, Vol. I (Madrid,
1861) pp. 39–40. In the Introduction (Madrid, 1883, part I), p. 144, Colmeiro
emphasizes that the king did not renounce any part of his sovereignty; he
conceded only the right of his subjects to give counsel in the Cortes. Julio
González in *Alfonso ix* (Madrid, 1944, p. 339, translates the last words by
"por cuyo corsejo se deberia negir."

7   *Comment by an Italian Historian on the*
Cortes of 1188

[p. 61] It is in Spain—with the great assembly of León in 1188
—that we find the first clear signs of the evolution of the old
concilios into true parliamentary institutions. . . .

[p. 62] As has been mentioned, the new elements in these as-

SOURCE. Antonio Marongiu, *Il Parlamento in Italia*, translated and adapted
by S. J. Woolf, *Medieval parliaments; a Comparative Study* (London, 1968),
pp. 62–63. Reprinted by permission of Eyre and Spottiswoode, London,
England.

semblies are visible only in the meeting of León in 1188. It was not simply the participation of representatives of the towns in the discussions and decisions taken there. After petitions had poured in from all sides, the king had summoned to his capital the archbishops, bishops, magnates and "chosen" of the cities. In all probability the protests were neither altruistic nor unco-ordinated. It is extremely likely that the mature citizens were responsible for some of them. The presence of "elected citizens" of the individual cities in these assemblies is wholly exceptional for the period. These facts, the new name of *curia* given to the assembly, and the extent of the concessions made by the king to the representatives of the country, support the hypothesis that the king did not act spontaneously (as even recent official historiography has asserted in the absence of reliable chronicles), but was forced to take and guarantee these decisions by a virtual coalition between the aristocracy and the cities.

There can be no doubt that the decisions taken in this *curia* were intended to create a new political constitution for the country; they were equivalent, in the modern sense of the word, to a constitutional charter, a *pacto politico civil*. This is demonstrated clearly by two of the decisions:

1. The undertaking given by the king to follow the counsels of his bishops, nobles and wise men in all circumstances in matters of peace and war;
2. The promise of the bishops (for ecclesiastics had been forbidden to take oaths by numerous councils since the eighth century) and the oath taken by the others (that is, the knights and citizens) to counsel the king faithfully for purposes of justice and peace.

Thus the necessary premises exist for us to assign this assembly to a higher level, legally and politically, than the preceding assemblies we have discussed, whether Spanish or of other countries.

[English]

8   *An American Historian on the Same*

With considerable exaggeration various authors have hailed the decrees promulgated by Alfonso IX at this time as a Leonese Magna Carta. The comparison is not entirely appropriate since Alfonso IX was not a tyrannical king whom rebellious barons were attempting to subordinate to the law of the land; nor is there any evidence that his decrees ever attained an importance and prestige in public law comparable to those of Magna Carta. Unlike the English charter, the decrees of 1188 were not confirmed explicitly by future monarchs upon accession to power, and later generations of Leonese or Castilians did not look back to the decrees of 1188 as the source of their liberties. On the other hand, Alfonso IX, like king John, acknowledged the existence of a body of law binding himself as well as his subjects. . . .

The decrees of 1188 were not the consequence of the concerted action of a hostile aristocracy attempting to impose its will upon the king; nor were they an abject capitulation to the townsmen angered by the prevailing disorders. They were, rather, proof of the king's determination to put an end to violence so that, in the words of Lucas of Túy, "he would be able to keep the kingdom in peace and justice." Alfonso IX pledged to uphold the law, to do justice to everyman, to punish evildoers, and to recover what rightfully belonged to the crown. His summons to the townsmen was an attempt to demonstrate his resolution and to use their support to counterbalance a turbulent nobility and to establish himself firmly in power.

[English]

SOURCE. Joseph F. O'Callaghan, "The Beginnings of the Cortes of León-Castile," in *A.H.R.* Vol. 74 (June, 1969) pp 1514–1515. Reprinted by permission of the author and of the American Historical Association, Washington, D.C., U.S.A.

CHAPTER III

THE CREATION OF PARLIAMENT IN THE THIRTEENTH CENTURY

Although there is still disagreement on the point, it seems probable that, by any reasonable definition, a parliament had emerged in most countries of Europe by the middle of the thirteenth century. As we shall see, it was accepted as an established institution by eminent statesmen by the third quarter of the century. At this point the problem of the nature of a parliament becomes very urgent. Our idea of what it was will deeply color our notion of how it finally came about. Reference has already been made to Bishop Stubbs' approach. That of his strongest critics in England is illustrated below by an extract from the writings of H. G. Richardson and G. O. Sayles.[1] In their view, parliament was in essence only an expanded session of the council. Many of its attributes were derived from its primary function of justice. G. O. Sayles said, it can be described as a court set above other courts. This view tends to make Richardson[2] and Sayles focus their attention on the thirteenth century when judicial activities in parliament became pronounced. In contrast, Stubbs emphasized the importance of developments in the earlier period, as far back as the Anglo-Saxon Witan.

European scholars such as Professor Marongiu have a view which is nearer to Stubbs than to Richardson and Sayles. As we have seen in the case of Professor Hintze, they find the creation of the parliamentary assembly as the end of a long process of evolution; and they believe that its essence was political in the broadest sense of the term. It is this approach which has been adopted below. Parliament, it will be argued, came into being,

---

[1] Document 11.

[2] For example in H. G. Richardson, "The Origins of Parliament," *Trans. Royal Hist. Soc.*, Vol. 11 (1938), pp. 137–185.

not primarily for judicial purposes, but for the co-operation of the king and the subjects in the most important business of the realm, including both politics and justice, but the former even more than the latter. Its significance is to be measured, not by the extent to which it facilitated the remedy of wrongs, but by the extent to which it enabled a new political cooperation to be achieved.

Two other criteria must be borne in mind. The first is the extent to which a particular assembly was "king-spun" in the sense that it had been created, and was continued, essentially to serve the needs and purposes of the king. If the idea of a cooperation between ruler and the community of the land, on something approaching equal terms, was lacking, no parliament was ever likely to thrive. The second criterion has to do with the attitude of the barons. To make a serious contribution to parliamentary development, they had to attend with a purpose broader than that of simply defending their own privileges. In order to have a wider support, they had to stand for the welfare of the kingdom as well as for their own advantage. Only on this basis, could they achieve an equilibrium in parliament which would be the basis of a spectacular advance.

Let us first consider the parliament of England. We shall find that it preeminently fulfilled the above criteria, and it had a great future before it. As far as we know, the first time that the general assembly was officially described as a parliament was in 1236. A certain Adam, representing the Chapter of Salisbury, pledged his faith to appear there; and this has somewhat questionably been regarded as showing that the gathering was an afforced session of the council. All we should conclude, perhaps, is that the term was firmly established in England very early in the reign of King Henry III.

In any case, the reference occurred at a time when there was bitter debate as to how England should be ruled. King Henry showed a tendency to consult only his familiars, and to minimize the need for the agreement of his magnates. In 1237, his barons protested that "all these things he had done without the counsel of his faithful subjects; nor ought they to share the penalty who had not shared the crime."[3] Both sides in the debate had a strong

[3] Document 1.

case. The magnates could point to close if often informal cooperation in the past. The king could argue that he had as
much right as any baron to choose his own advisers and to consult them about any affair that he chose. The debate involved
primarily the "privy" council, but it was obviously also concerned
with the general sessions of the *Curia*.

The baronial claim to give agreement to weighty business un-
dertaken by the king was first put forward in a scheme of reform
in 1244.[4] The scheme is now referred to as a "Paper Constitution"
because it was not accepted by King Henry III. The barons tried
to ensure a right to assent, not in the general assembly, but in
the king's small council, perhaps because they felt that the affairs
of both the king and kingdom were being decided there. They
proposed that four of them should be present, to be called conservators of liberties. They were not to be removed without common consent. These four should "treat" concerning important
decisions. They should also hear the complaints of individuals,
and remedy wrongs. The collective body of prelates and barons
was to meet when necessary and at their own request. The magnates clearly distinguished between the general assembly and the
king's council. They evidently believed that they could achieve
in the latter the kind of cooperation with the king which Henry
denied them in the former. In this, they were mistaken, but their
effort shows how urgent in their eyes the problem of political cooperation had become. Their plan was bold and ingenious, but
its fusion of the functions of the "privy" council and the general
session of the *Curia* was quite unacceptable to the ruler and was
in any case not practicable. Thirteenth-century administrative
genius, in the end, produced its remarkable results by dividing
and not by uniting the great and small councils, and by clinging
to the former, and not attempting to exploit the latter, as the
supreme place of cooperation with the king.

Thus Henry III rejected the bold proposals of 1244, and they
were never repeated. Fourteen years later, the reformers worked
through both the small council on the one hand and the parliamentary assembly on the other; but the "treating" took place in

4 Document 2. For important comments on the views of the barons at this
time, see C. M. Radding, "The Origins of Bracton's *Addicio de Cartis*,"
Speculum Vol. 44 (April, 1969), pp. 239–246.

the latter. In the famous Provisions of Oxford of 1258, the barons elected magnates to the council and at the same time set down that council and magnates should "treat" together in parliament which should be summoned at least three times a year. The only reason why all the great lords were not to be summoned to the assembly was to save expense. The barons who did attend may have regarded themselves as representing, or at least speaking on behalf of, the community of all the land.[5] The "treaty" which took place was to concern the affairs of both the kingdom and the king. The Provisions of Oxford dominated the relations of the king and his subjects for the whole period 1258–65 and left an indelible mark on the constitution.

It has, indeed, been argued that they were not intended to describe the function of parliament, and that therefore their wording is irrelevant to the problem of what parliament was thought to be in 1258; but it is hard to take this suggestion very seriously. The current opinion of parliament could not possibly fail to be reflected in a document of such importance, even if the institution was distorted to serve the purpose of baronial reform. The document had much more than temporary significance; it also incidentally revealed the deepest political ideals of one of the most inspiring reforming movements in English history. Its effects continued long after Simon de Montfort's death and the triumph of his opponents. It has been calculated that "sixteen or seventeen assemblies that can be described as parliaments had been gathered together in England between the battle of Evesham (1265) and the death of Henry III (1272).[6]

It was probably no accident that there were important references to parliament, made by well-known publicists shortly after the struggle of 1258–1265. In 1269, Thomas Wykes, an English chronicler, recorded how "the king and the magnates treated about the business of the king and the kingdom as was their wont, in the manner of parliament;[7] and in 1271 Walter Giffard, archbishop of York, commented:

[5] Cf. T. P. Taswell-Langmead, *English Constitutional History*, Tenth edition, revised by T. F. T. Plucknett (London, 1946), p. 149.

[6] F. M. Powicke, *The Thirteenth Century*, p. 341.

[7] *Annales Monastici*, edited by H. R. Luard (R. S. 1869), Vol. IV, p. 227. Thomas probably wrote after 1282.

"We should aim at more parliaments to mitigate the anger of the times, to reconcile discords, and to procure matters of peace as best we may by ordinance of the realm."[8]

Parliament was as familiar to him as it was to Thomas. He believed that it dealt with high politics, and that its ordinances were those of the realm, which we may venture to guess meant that they were the product of both the king and the community.

On the continent, Humbert de Romans, General of the Dominican Order, made a similar reference in a book called "Concerning the Learning of the Preachers," which was intended to help Dominican friars in their work. The fact that this work might include preaching before parliament proves that the institution was well recognized. Humbert saw three ingredients in such an assembly: the king, the magnates, and the councillors. Its business was general, both judicial and political. Exactly how it was to be disposed of Humbert does not say; it was probably difficult to generalize, and in any case there was no need to do so for the purpose he had in mind. But his words show clearly that parliaments were a European phenomenon.

They serve to raise the question, which unfortunately we cannot answer, of how far the events in England between 1258 and 1265 affected opinion and practice on the Continent. It is hard not to think that they had a far-reaching influence. The issues raised in the English struggle must have aroused much interest and attention abroad; and St. Louis made the conflict still more notable by his famous arbitration. Both Henry III and Simon de Montfort were well-known, especially in France. Guy, son of Simon made the conflict between the two even more familiar by murdering Henry of Almain in a church at Viterbo during Mass, an action which shocked the European aristocracy.

However, in his references to parliaments, Humbert may possibly have had the great Imperial assemblies particularly in mind, though these were very different from those of England, or even of France.

A good many of them are referred to in the chronicles, but they do not seem to show the Emperor as seeking anything more binding from his subjects than advice. In 1084, for example,

---

[8] *Historical Papers and Letters from Northern Registers,* edited by J. Raine (R. S. 1873), p. 36.

the Emperor Henry IV summoned a general *colloquium* and said that he would not undertake an expedition he had in mind "until what was to be done had been considered in common counsel." In 1119, Henry V told pope Calixtus II that he could not decide an important question without a general *colloquium* of the princes of the Empire; and Frederick Barbarossa made a similar statement in 1159. Lothar III promulgated a constitution at Roncaglia in 1136 "following the exhortation and counsel of the prelates, nobles, and city magistrates." A diet held there by Frederick Barbarossa in 1154 was described by a chronicler as a *parlamentum*. But in all these assemblies the Emperor took counsel; he did not "treat." Nor can we see any clear transition from counsel to "treaty." In Frederick Barbarossa's famous assembly at Roncaglia in Italy, in 1158, the first plenary session was preceded by four days of discussion in which all present freely advanced opinions. Then the Emperor made an opening address and others followed in order of precedence "according to Italian custom." The Imperial claim to appoint the chief officials of the north Italian cities and to impose taxes was declared by four famous doctors of Bologna to be in accordance with Roman Law. Those present unanimously agreed. Even in regard to these most weighty matters there was no genuine "treaty." Nor did one ever develop. One reason for this seems to be revealed in the declaration by the archbishop of Milan: "Know that the whole of the people's right to make laws has been granted to you [i.e. to the Emperor]." The influence of such a view may possibly be seen in the most famous pronouncement concerning legislation, which was made in 1231 by Henry VII, King of the Romans and son of the Emperor Frederick II.

In that year, Henry who had been given the rule over Germany during his father's absence in Italy, issued a momentous concession to the German magnates. It was called the *Constitutio in Favorem Principum*, and it gave them almost complete judicial and military independence. At the same time, however, he issued an Edict of Wörms,[9] whose meaning is not so clear. In it, he said that he had been requested to give a ruling on the making of new laws, and when the agreement of the princes had been

9 Document 5.

asked, he defined the procedure. He declared that territorial lords
could not make any constitutions or new laws unless the consent
of the greater and better men of their territory had first been
obtained.

The exact significance of this edict is uncertain. As Professor
Mitteis argues,[10] it must almost certainly be regarded as complementary to the *Constitutio*. Nearly all historians seem to agree,
however, that Henry intended it to provide some curb on the
growth of princely power which was now inevitable. We may accept this view; but it seems to lead us to some very interesting observations. It has been claimed that the principle recognized by the
Edict was that princes ought to rule only with the consent of their
subjects, and this again is true. But the way in which this principle was expressed is significant. A prince, Henry decreed, had to
get the consent of the better and greater men of his territory.
But this did not, apparently, mean that these men had to agree to
what the prince ordained; they had only to agree that he should
ordain. This was in strict accord with the Imperial tradition as
declared by the Archbishop of Milan in the words above. Thus,
even though King Henry wished to put a brake on the growing
power of the territorial lords, he actually worded his decree so as
to provide them with a procedure which might powerfully limit
the participation of the better and greater men in the making of
constitutions and new laws. Despite the air of liberalism in his
decree, he guaranteed such lords forever (unless they themselves
abrogated them) the privileges they had received in the *Constitutio in Favorem Principum*, a not inconsiderable gain. Henry
may have worded his Edict under compulsion from the lords, but
of this we cannot be certain. As is well known, it did not prevent
the development of parliaments in the princely states; but we
cannot say how much it contributed to their growth.

It is true that even the Emperors were not unaffected by new
ideas of cooperation with their subjects. Frederick II himself
summoned an Imperial assembly at Mainz in 1235, in order to
promulgate a *Constitutio Pacis* with the assent as well as the
counsel of the princes. But the Imperial tradition proved too
stubborn for this to become a decisive precedent. In any case, the

10 Document 6.

Imperial Diet gradually declined into impotence, destroyed by the centrifugal tendencies of the princes. It never became pre-eminent, in spite of the Imperial prestige.

Such conclusions may only be drawn from the wording of the Edict of Wörms if we regard this concession as being just as precise and nicely calculated as that of Alfonso IX, or of Magna Carta, or of Frederick II in 1232; and the same is probably true if we compare it with the concession of Peter III of Aragon in 1283. Most probably, the rulers of Europe were conscious of the emergence of new problems in the old cooperation between kings and subjects in the making of laws. They reacted each in his own way, governed by history and tradition and the circumstances of their day. In this as in many other political responses to the challenges of history, power and glory are not always the best guarantee of success. The English kings learned more from adversity than the Emperors from their claim to be the vicars of God.

Humbert de Romans would no doubt also be familiar with striking developments of the general *Curia* which occurred in Sicily under Frederick II, roughly at the same time as King Henry VII's Edict at Wörms. Such a *Curia* was held at San Germano as early as 1208, and it may have witnessed agreement on common action, though what form this agreement took is obscure. Professor Marongiu says that Frederick imposed a tax in 1231 on the basis of counsel and a "corresponding vote"; though elsewhere he quotes words describing the procedure as being only "by the counsel of the prelates, counts, barons and many citizens." His general conclusion is that Frederick was not in sympathy with the sentiments which had been expressed by his son at Wörms in 1231; he wanted to be lord of everyone and everything in the kingdom of Sicily. This opinion may be borne out by the summons he issued directing the attendance of men from cities and castles at an assembly to be held at Foggia in 1232. We do not know whether or not the magnates were invited to "treat"; but the lesser people, at least, were only to attend "for the utility of the realm and the common good."[11]

Again to quote Professor Marongiu, a writ of summons in 1240 invited the subjects to an assembly only to contemplate the

[11] Chapter IV, Document 1.

majesty and serenity of the sovereign and to hear his words. Later the Angevin kings who ruled Sicily after the fall of the Hohenstauffen line probably continued this attitude. Pope Clement IV advised Charles of Anjou, the first of them, to obtain both counsel and consent from the magnates and community for his taxation; but as far as we know Charles largely ignored this advice. In Sicily, as in Germany itself, there were conflicting tendencies, but as head of the Holy Roman Empire, Frederick II stood, in the final analysis, for a political tradition which was hostile to parliamentary growth. He accepted consultation and even, on occasions, the need for agreement between ruler and subjects on important matters. But it seems likely that he was only trying to turn to his own purpose the forces which were stirring all over the West; and with which he was perfectly familiar through his diplomatic contacts, especially with the English king, Henry III. What he would have done, had he lived longer, it is impossible to say.

Elsewhere in Italy circumstances were similarly inimical to the growth of parliaments. Pope Innocent III summoned general assemblies in the Papal States, in 1200 and 1207, similar to those summoned by Frederick; but it is doubtful if the vicar of Christ had ideas about such assemblies which differed greatly from those of the Emperor, vicar of God. This seems to be true even though there are clear signs of rule by agreement in 1270-1 and 1298. In Northern Italy, other forms of consultation and agreement were worked out in the city states. For very diverse reasons, Italy, despite her great traditions and early promise, was not to be a pioneer of the medieval parliament.

If we turn from Italy to Spain, it becomes evident that, despite the important assembly of 1188, the Spanish kingdoms also were probably not destined to remain in the forefront of parliamentary development. The next great landmark there was delayed until 1283, when King Peter III of Aragon, bidding for the support of his subjects in his war against the Angevins, summoned an assembly of Catalonia to meet at Barcelona.[12] Prelates, barons, knights and citizens were summoned. In the name of themselves and all the community of Catalonia, they made certain requests and petitions to the king which Peter granted. He promised that

12 Document 7.

in the future any ruler who wished to issue general constitutions or statutes in Catalonia would do so with the approval and consent of the prelates and other orders. Some historians have taken this to mean the *previous* consent, as in the concession of Henry VII in Germany.[13] In order to do this, they have had to depart from the original text.[14] They may be closer to the spirit, if not the letter, of Peter's concession; but it is impossible to make a judgement on this point without a major research effort.

Peter also conceded that he would hold a general *Curia* once a year, unless circumstances prevented, to "treat" about the state and reform of the kingdom, and there seems to be no ambiguity about this fact. Spanish kings and subjects were perfectly familiar with the process of treating together in a Cortes, as may be seen by even a cursory survey of the records of Aragon and León-Castile, and by the writings of Julio Gonzalez and Nilda Guglielmi.[15] They were accustomed to enactments "by common counsel and assent." Thus, when Peter promised to treat about the kingdom, he was making a weighty concession; but the reform was apparently only to affect the kingdom and not the king.

Finally, Peter also made an important grant to nobles and citizens called the Union. He conceded that the Cortes would be summoned once a year in Saragossa, and that he would take counsel with the Cortes before he made war or peace. But he only promised to take counsel; and this was no more than what Alfonso of León had conceded in 1188.[16] Shortly afterwards, his son granted further that the Cortes should have the right of judgement where the king himself was involved, and that his councillors should be chosen by the Cortes from among its members. He also conceded, finally, that his subjects had a right to rebel, electing some other to be their king if he did not keep his word.

These concessions have been regarded with some justice as the birth certificate of the Catalan parliament. They can hardly be paralleled in any other state. But we have to make one important reservation. There was an emphasis on counsel rather than agreement, and treating between king and Cortes was not said to affect

13 This is discussed on pp. 64–65 above.

14 See p. 83 below, note 1.

15 Document 9.

16 Document 6.

royal power. As in the German declaration at Wörms, the significance of such distinctions is obviously debatable. Nevertheless, the precedent of 1231 provides a strong argument for believing that the distinctions had constitutional significance. They suggest a tacit assumption that the king's prerogative was above the reach of legislation, that may be compared with a similar attitude on the part of Edward II of England in a famous but ineffective statute of 1322. Thus the kings of Aragon, unlike those of England, were probably able to preserve the innermost keep of their authority intact.

A reflection of their exaltation of the royal power may perhaps be seen in Peter III's description of his subjects as begging him humbly, on bended knees, to grant their petition, even if his words have to be taken with a grain of salt. However, he may have kept his high royal pretensions but in fact have surrendered some of the reality of his power. This did, in fact, happen in León-Castile.[17]

On the whole, it seems likely, however, that in spite of the concessions by Peter III and his son, the kings of Aragon continued to be inspired by the traditions of the Reconquest. In the end, the powers of the Cortes would be destroyed by these traditions, and by the authority that the kings retained, in 1283 and at other times. The stubborn traditions of royal power would be expanded in the great days of the sixteenth century by rulers who stood for the unity of Spain, and for the aspirations of a proud and successful people who were busily exploring and exploiting a new world.

France, as is well known, was late in developing the institutions of government, including parliament. The great expansion of the royal domain, which would contribute to this, did not occur until the reign of Philip Augustus (1180–1223), and even Philip, though he did indulge in "perpetual parleys" with his barons, did not find it necessary to seek frequent baronial aids. His successor, Louis VIII (1223–1226), had occasion to call a good many more assemblies, but the next ruler Louis IX (St. Louis, 1226–1270) would not, or could not, follow this example. Important magnates even refused to attend his coronation; and parleys with his barons were infrequent in his early years. Even later, Louis IX

17 Document 9.

ruled with a paternal devotion to the welfare of his people, rather than in cooperation with his barons by means of frequent general assemblies. No doubt he was influenced by the practical difficulties of distance and lack of homogeneity in France. But one consequence of his policy and his prestige was that by the end of the thirteenth century the French monarchy had become strong, and the general assembly of the *Curia* had tended to become correspondingly weak.

Philip the Fair (1285–1314) began a new period in the history of this assembly by summoning the famous States-General of 1302. His purpose was clearly to get a general support from his subjects in a momentous clash with pope Boniface VIII. In 1301, Philip had arrested Bernard Saisset, bishop of Pamiers, and the pope not only condemned this act but also challenged the whole right of a ruler to exercise secular authority so as to destroy the traditional freedoms of the church. In this vitally important conflict of powers, Philip summoned both magnates and representatives of the towns to inform them of the issues and to gain their support. He wanted, he said, to discuss with them arduous matters which concerned his Estate and liberty, and also the liberty of his churches and prelates, of his nobles, and of every inhabitant of the land. Words attributed to Pierre Flotte and addressed to the King indicate the nature of the support Philip received:

"We beg you as master and friend to help us defend the liberty of the realm and of the church."

Olivier-Martin believed that this was a new institution. Professor Marongiu has claimed that it expressed the substance of the famous tag from Justinian's Code used earlier by the English King Edward I: "What touches all should be approved by all." Professor Fawtier believed that the assembly of 1302 was not the first meeting of the Estates-General; it was better than that. It was a direct consultation of the public opinion of France without intermediaries; the king for the first time took up a position on a matter of general policy, but wished to know after he had taken his stand if this was accepted and approved by all his subjects.

In attempting to decide the significance of the assembly, we have to assume that Philip the Fair knew a great deal about the striking developments which had already taken place elsewhere.

He was, in fact, one of the best advised rulers in Europe.[18] His decisions in 1302 were much too important to have been taken without careful thought. It is significant therefore that in his writs for the assembly, Philip did not summon his magnates merely to give counsel or to hear his decisions; he summoned them "to deliberate and treat."[19] By 1302, the word *tractare* was heavy with associations. It had become familiar by a generation of usage in nearby England, where it was standard in the parliamentary writ of summons. Nor was this all. Lesser men also were summoned to treat and deliberate, although stress was laid on their duty also "to hear, to receive and to do." Pierre Flotte in his rhetoric did not offer counsel or acclamation; he offered partnership in a common endeavour.

It seems likely that, faced with a severe crisis, Philip drew on precedents which had helped rulers to obtain political unity elsewhere. Doubtless he drew particularly on the example of England, where, in his own quarrel with the Pope, Edward I had worked hard to obtain not only the counsel but also the agreement of all his people in parliament.

There are therefore reasons for thinking that in calling the assembly of 1302. Philip was taking a cautious step in the same direction as King Edward I. His experiment seems to have been very successful. It is not surprising that he summoned a similar assembly in 1308. Indeed, there is evidence of a parallel development in nearby Brabant, where duke John II in 1312 granted a charter to his subjects in which he promised that all new laws and amendments would be made only with the advice and consent of an assembly of nobles and citizens. The powers of the Brabant assembly were extended during the next few years until in 1356 the assembly of nobles and citizens received control over war, alliances, ducal appointments, legislation, and taxation.[20]

[18] J. R. Strayer, "Philip the Fair—A "Constitutional King," in *A.H.R.*, Vol. 62 (1956), pp. 18–32; B. Lyon, "What made a Medieval King Constitutional?," in *Essays in Medieval History Presented to Bertie Wilkinson* (Toronto, 1969), pp. 157–175.

[19] See the documents discovered by C. H. Taylor, translated in part Chapter IV, Document 4.

[20] Bryce Lyon, "Medieval Constitutionalism: a Balance of Power," in *Studies Presented to the International Commission for the History of Representative and Parliamentary Institutions*, Vol. 24 (1961) pp. 155–183.

It looks as though, in relation to Philip the Fair's Estates-General, we shall have to modify slightly Professor Fawtier's conclusion. The assembly was a landmark, not because the king wanted to know if his subjects accepted and approved of a stand he had already taken; but rather because in view of the unforeseeable contingencies which might arise in his quarrel, he sought some kind of partnership with them, though he wanted this on his own terms. The assembly of 1302 was a genuine parliament, and thus constituted a landmark; but it was basically "king-spun." It was set up on the king's initiative and to serve his purpose. It was not calculated to fire the imagination of Frenchmen as did those in which subjects could feel that they were fully accepted as sharing with the monarch the disposal of the highest affairs of the realm. Finally, the timing was important. The French assembly came after an important expansion of the power of the ruler, whereas the first important steps in Spain and England had come as early as 1188 and when the king, in some respects, was not so strong.

The limited faith of the French magnates in the newly formulated concept of the Estates-General was clearly revealed in the famous revolt of 1314–1316. This was plainly a movement to safeguard aristocratic and local privilege, not to obtain a greater cooperation with the king in the general assembly. In fact, it can be argued that the French people, both nobles and commoners, deliberately turned away from that assembly. They must have known, or at least some of their leaders must have known, how the English had made claims for parliament under Edward I, and how they had made parliament central in their demands on Edward II in the famous Ordinances of 1311. England and France were still very close, and a daughter of the French king Philip the Fair was queen of England. But, for whatever reason, the French magnates rejected the English example, and their rejection may well be regarded as a turning point in French history.

The distrust of the States-General increased the importance of the regional assemblies. These had been summoned in France from at least the third quarter of the thirteenth century; those of Languedoc had met, for example, in 1269, 1271, and 1275. They were strengthened, not weakened, by the revolts of 1314–1316, as witnessed by the Charter to the Normans in 1315. They were a poor substitute for a strong central assembly, and provided an ineffective limitation on the power of the king. The king looked to them for consultation rather than agreement. In any case, agreement was easier to get from them than from the central assembly. In 1319, King Philip V took steps to obtain from assemblies of nobles in seven localities a grant of a subsidy which had been refused in a large assembly in Paris.

Both the king and the magnates in the end, and for different reasons, preferred the local to the central assembly, even though both lent the Estates-General support in 1302 and 1308. This fact shows more clearly perhaps, than any other, the difference between the political and constitutional conditions in which the parliamentary assembly developed in two neighbouring countries that were so closely related in their history and traditions.

In all the countries of Europe, it seems possible to conclude, there was a great political ferment throughout the thirteenth century, and a general development of a new and profoundly important institution. In this development, the two greatest centres of influence were England and Germany, representing at bottom two very different concepts of political authority. The latter was permeated by the Imperial tradition which proved to be so strong that it could not be reconciled successfully with Germanic and feudal notions of limited royal power. The former, despite the strength of the monarchy, was permeated by notions of cooperation between the king and his people on every level of society, so powerful that attempts to ignore them gave rise to great movements of the baronage by which they succeeded in placing permanent limitations on the royal authority.

The two different concepts can be seen inspiring to a greater or lesser degree all the major parliamentary assemblies of Europe. It is almost certain that the rulers of the West had the examples of England and Germany before them as they grappled with their own problems. France and Spain stood midway between the extremes. A number of French and Spanish rulers tried to make the best of both worlds, wishing to develop parliamentary rule, while keeping the essence of their authority unimpaired. They wished to use the new political consciousness of their people, and to harness it to the power of their central government, but not to accept a genuine partnership with the community of their realm. They achieved some temporary triumphs, and prepared the way for an age of glory and expansion in the modern period; but they did not succeed in transmitting to that period the genuine feudal tradition of government subject to God and the law, by agreement between the kings and the community of the realm, even if this were represented only by a gathering of the greater lords.

Despite all the divergence of growth, it must still be insisted that the great concept of parliament, as the means of reconciling liberty and order in a large territorial state, was a product of the whole *Respublica Christiana*. In the common act of creation which embraced the whole of a civilization, England owed as much as she gave. We shall never be able to disentangle the reciprocal influences which were at work, and we should be very foolish to assign credit or blame for success or failure. Circumstances varied widely. The factors influencing what we have described above as a political miracle were so evenly balanced that even a touch of adversity was enough to destroy the chance of ultimate success. In spite of that, thirteenth-century kings and magnates were able to hand on to posterity one of the most effective political institutions of all time.

It must be added, finally, that the acceptance of a parliamentary partnership in government was only the beginning of the political experiment, though here, as often elsewhere, the first step is all-important. The experiment would not be complete until all the people, not only the magnates, had found a place in the assembly. The story of this process would take us far beyond the Middle Ages. Nevertheless its beginnings must be touched upon, for it was the acceptance of representatives of the community beyond the circle of the lords and prelates which gave the final assurance of success to the experiment of the thirteenth century. It ensured that the combination of king and magnates in the new institution would not lead to a sterile oligarchy in which both united to exploit the unprivileged community. It meant that there would not evolve a constitution in which liberty was confined to the comparative few who had a place in the parliamentary system.

Thus, the adoption of representation, and the acceptance of the participation of small gentry and citizens in the communities of the kingdoms, were almost as great an achievement as the creation of parliamentary cooperation and partnership. It cannot be dealt with at any length or its great complexities unravelled; but it is so important and interesting that it must be discussed, however briefly, in the final chapter below.

1   An English General Assembly of 1237

In the year of our lord 1237 [1236] . . . the king held his court at Christmas in Winchester. He immediately sent royal letters throughout all the land of England, and he commanded all those belonging to the realm of England, namely archbishops, bishops, abbots, and priors who had been installed, earls and barons, that they should all, without exception, meet on the Octave of Epiphany at London, to treat about royal business which concerned the whole realm. When they heard this, the magnates immediately obeyed the royal command; they believed they were going to settle imperial or other arduous affairs. Thus, on the day of St. Hilary an infinite multitude of magnates gathered in London, namely all the *universitas* of the realm. When, they had sat down together, in the royal palace at Westminster, to hear the will of the king, William of Ralegh, a clerk and "familiar" of the king, arose in their midst. He was a discreet man and learned in the law of the land. He rose so that, like a mediator between the king and the magnates of the realm, he might make public the royal intention and will.

He spoke as follows: "The king proclaims to you that whatever he has done hitherto, from this moment henceforth he will subject himself without question to the counsels of you all, as his faithful and natural men. Truly, those who up to this time were keepers of his treasure, treating of his business, have rendered a false account of all the money they have received. Wherefore, the lord king is now entirely denuded of money without which any king is desolate. He humbly requests an aid of money; this money

SOURCE. Translated by B. Wilkinson, in *The Constitutional History of England 1216–1399*, Vol. 3 (London, 1958) pp. 297–299, from Matthew Paris, *Chronica Majora*, edited by H. R. Luard (R. S., 1872) Vol. 3, pp. 380–384. Reprinted by permission of the Longman Group, Harlow, England.

to be collected to your clear satisfaction, according to the disposition of some of your members chosen for this purpose, and to be kept for expenditure to meet the indispensable needs of the kingdom, . . ."

And the magnates replied in indignation that they had been burdened in every manner, and often, by the promise and payment, now of a twentieth, now of a thirtieth and now of a fiftieth. They declared that it would be too shameful and harmful to allow a king (who was so easily led astray, and who never repelled or affrighted any one, even the least, of the enemies of the kingdom, nor ever extended the bounds of the kingdom, but made them less and subjected them to aliens) to extort by his arguments so much money, so often and in such quantities, from his native subjects, as if from serfs of the lowest estate, to their detriment and to the advantage of foreigners. When the king heard this, he wished to quieten this general murmur. He promised on oath that he would never more exasperate the nobles of the realm by injury or grieve them, if only they would of their favour grant and pay a thirtieth part of the moveable goods of England. For, as he said, he had greatly diminished his treasury a little while before by sending a great deal of money to the emperor for the marriage of his sister; and again he had diminished it for his own marriage.

To which, it was replied, not silently, that he [Henry] had done all these things without the counsel of his faithful; nor should they share the punishment who were not involved in the crime.

At length the magnates retired to a more secret place apart, so that . . . they might take counsel together in considering the manner and quantity of the aid which was demanded. When they went apart Gilbert Bassett, less circumspect than he ought to have been in his speech, said the following words to the king in the common hearing. "My Lord king, will you send one of your own people to be present with them in the colloquy of your barons." He was seated, when he uttered these words, a few places away from the side of the king. To whom, for the other side, Richard Percy replied—he had been present at the colloquy of the magnates, and he was offended, not without cause—"What is this that you have said, friend Gilbert? Are we aliens and not the king's friends?" Thus Gilbert was reproved for his rude and unexpected words. . . . And thus, with very many debates the colloquy was extended by a delay of four days. [The king then made many concessions, including a promise to confirm Magna Carta and the addition of magnates to the king's council, and the thirtieth was granted.]

[Latin]

2   An English "Paper Constitution" of 1244

. . . let four be elected by common assent, who have power and rank, from amongst the more discreet of the whole realm, who shall be of the king's council and sworn that they will faithfully "treat" concerning the business of the lord king and of the realm, and will give justice to all without any regarding of persons. These four shall follow the lord king, and if not all of them, at least two shall always be present, so that they may hear the complaints of each person and will be able to give speedy succour to those suffering wrong. The treasury of the lord king is to be "treated" with their inspection and knowledge; and the money which has been specially granted by all, for the benefit of the lord king and of the kingdom, shall be spent as they shall see to be the most advantageous. And they shall be conservators of liberties. And as they are elected with the assent of all, so none of them can be removed without common assent. . . . And the *universitas* shall not meet again without them, but shall meet when it shall be necessary and at their instance.

[Latin]

SOURCE. Translated, with comments, by B. Wilkinson, in *The Constitutional History of England, 1216–1399*, Vol. I (London, 1948), pp. 129–130. Reprinted by permission of the Longman Group, Harlow, England. The passage was taken from Matthew Paris' *Chronica Majora*, edited by H. R. Luard (R. S. 1872), Vol. 4, pp. 362–368.

3   References to Parliament in the English Provisions of Oxford in 1258

Concerning the parliaments, as to how many shall be held annually and in what manner:—It should be remembered that the twenty-four [elected to reform the state of the kingdom] have ordained that there are to be three parliaments a year: the first on the octave of St. Michael, the second on the morrow of Candlemas, and the third on the first day of June, that is to say, three weeks before [the feast of] St. John.

To these three parliaments the chosen councillors of the king shall come, even if they are not summoned, in order to examine the state of the kingdom and to "treat" about the common needs of the kingdom and likewise of the king; and by the king's command [they shall come] also at other times, whenever it is necessary.

So too it should be remembered that the community is to elect twelve good men who shall come to the three parliaments and at other times, when there is need and when the king and his council summon them to "treat" about the affairs of the king and the kingdom.

And [it has been decided] that the community shall hold as established whatever these twelve shall do—and this is to reduce the cost to the community. . . .

[French]

SOURCE. Translated with comments by B. Wilkinson, *Constitutional History*, as above, Vol. I, p. 170. Reprinted by permission of the Longman Group, Harlow, England. The passage was from the *Annals of Burton*, in *Annales Monastici*, edited by H. R. Luard (R. S., 1864), Vol. I, 378–384.

4   *The Reference to Parliament in the English
Legal Treatise* Fleta, *of the Reign
of Edward I*

Concerning the different kinds of King's courts.

The king has, for instance, his court in his council in his parliaments, there being present prelates, earls, barons, magnates and other skilled men; and there are terminated doubts concerning judgements, and new remedies are devised for new wrongs which have arisen, and justice is done to each one according to his deserts.

[Latin]

SOURCE. Translated in my *Constitutional History* as above, Vol. 3 (London, 1958) p. 170. From *Fleta,* edited and translated by H. G. Richardson and G. O. Sayles, Selden Society, Vol. 72 (London, 1955), Vol. 2, p. 109.

5   *The Declaration of Henry VII, King of
the Romans, at Wörms, on
1 May, 1231*

Henry, by the Grace of God King of the Romans and forever august, sends to all the faithful people of his empire his grace and good will. We desire everyone to know that at a solemn diet held in our presence at Wörms we were asked that a ruling be given on the question of whether or not a territorial lord can make any constitution or new law without any consultation with the better and greater men of his territory. When the agreement of the princes had been asked, the matter was defined in this way. Neither princes nor others may make any constitutions or new laws unless the consent of the better and greater men of the territory has first been obtained. We have therefore caused these

SOURCE. *Sentententia de iure statuum terrae,* in *Monumenta Germaniae Historica,* Legum IV, Constitutiones II (Hanover, 1896), number 305, p. 420.

present letters to be written and furnished with our seal, to give this sentence the strength of perpetual validity.

Given at Wörms, on 1 May, 1231.

[Latin]

6   The German Historian, Heinrich Mitteis, on the Declaration at Wörms

On the same day that Henry [VII] granted the princes the *Statutum in favorem principum* [statute in favour of the princes], he forbade them, by imperial decree, to impose any new service on their subjects without the consent of the greater and better men of the land. Both decrees must have been complementary to each other, and should be interpreted together. The king perhaps hoped in this way to be able to prevent an overquick increase in the power of the princes: he wished to place the territorial lords between two fires, just as Conrad II had done in the case of the crown vassals by the decree of 1037. The resulting relationship between the territorial lords and the Estates varied greatly, and we cannot examine every particular case. In some states, such as Mecklenburg, the Estates played a part in the constitution until 1918. In others, especially in Prussia, the dualism of prince and Estates was set aside, a process helped by the superiority of the princes in the means of war, above all in more modern times in artillery.

[German]

SOURCE. Heinrich Mitteis, *Der Staat des Hohen Mittelalters* (Weimar, 1962) p. 361. Translated by permission of H. Böhlaus, Weimar, Germany.

7   *Concessions in the Cortes of Aragon by*
           King Peter III, in 1283

And each and every one of the aforesaid [this refers to the nobles, barons, knights and citizens who were present, some of whom were enumerated] requested that we would deign to give our assent to, and freely concede, certain petitions and articles that are to be ordained and declared, as can be perceived in our constitutions and ordinances, and in other matters on each article, written below. They begged us humbly in the following manner:

It pertains to the royal excellency to concede liberties and immunities to subjects, and also to approve and inviolably observe the privileges granted to them by his ancestors, as well as the established customs and good observances. Therefore, we the prelates, barons, citizens and men of the towns, of Catalonia beg on bended knees and as humbly as we can, in the name of ourselves and of all the community (*universitas*) of Catalonia, that you the most illustrious lord king will deign freely to accept, concede, and approve the petitions and articles below, as these tend to your honour and the general good estate of Catalonia.

We the king have viewed the aforesaid supplications, petitions, and articles. We have taken counsel about them and have examined them diligently. And we have considered the fact that it is an attribute of the royal dignity that a king should watch over the welfare of his subjects and keep his land in peace; and he should endow his faithful and deserving subjects with their immunities, liberties and franchises to be observed unimpaired . . . [the king remarks on the good faith, right counsel, favour and help which the subjects gave to his ancestors] therefore, on behalf of ourself and of ours, we restore, concede, and approve . . . .

[clause IX] Item, we decree, wish and ordain that if we or any successor shall wish to enact any general constitution or any statute in Catalonia, we shall do so with the approval and consent of the prelates, barons, knights and citizens of Catalonia or,

SOURCE. *Cortes de los Antiguos Reinos de Aragon y Principado de Cataluna,* pub. by La Real Academia de la Historia, Vol. I, part I (Madrid, 1896), pp. 144–153.

when these have been summoned, that of the greater and wiser part.

[clause XVIII] Item, once a year, at a time most expedient for us, we and our successors will hold our general Catalonian *Curia* in which we shall "treat" concerning the good state and reform of the land, together with the prelates, barons, knights, citizens and men of the towns; but we shall not be bound to celebrate or hold the *Curia* if any just cause shall prevent us.

[clauses XIX to L are omitted]

These things were enacted in a general *Curia* as above, there being present [the subjects enumerated above], who asked and humbly petitioned.

[Latin]

8   An Italian Historian's View of the Concessions made by Peter III of Aragon, in 1283

[The cortes had been summoned to treat of the good state and order of the country] "On bended knees," as the parliamentary vote states, but with the self-consciousness and explicit assumption of their quality of representatives of the entire Catalan people (*nomine suo et tocius universitatis Catalonie*), the participants laid before the king "a petition and request" that he confirm and guarantee all the liberties and privileges of his subjects. The king, in his preamble, enunciated the formula—so common in analagous circumstances—of the duty of sovereigns to watch over the good of their subjects and to reward them for their fealty, and expressed his gratitude for the sacrifices they had made; he then formally accepted the parliamentary votes. He promulgated a whole series of legislative decrees to guarantee both the rights of his subjects and an upright administration,

SOURCE. Antonio Marongiu, *Il Parlamento In Italia Nel Medio Evo E Nell' Età Moderna* (Milan, 1962) translated and adapted by S. J. Woolf, under the title *Medieval Parliaments, A Comparative Study* (London, 1968), pp. 68–69. Reprinted by permission of A. B. P. International and of Eyre and Spottiswoode (Publishers Ltd.)

especially in matters of taxation and justice. . . . The underlying motive for this remarkable innovation was the government's financial weakness, because of its need to wage war against the Angevins following the conquest of Sicily.

What is of particular interest for the purpose of our study is that on this occasion the king also made a double promise and declaration, which was regarded as possessing the authority of a legislative measure. On the one hand, he promised that henceforth sovereigns would not issue general constitutions or statutes in Catalonia without the previous[1] deliberation and consent of the prelates, barons, knights and citizens, or of the majority (*greater and wiser part*) of the members of appropriate assemblies. On the other hand, he declared that, unless legitimately hindered, the king would hold a general curia of the Catalans once a year on a date and location to be determined each time. It is interesting to note that the Catalan text of the constitution was traditionally called by the Catalan word for once a year: *una vegada lo any*. The purpose of the meeting, to be attended by the clergy, aristocracy and men of the *ville*, was to treat of the good state of the kingdom and all necessary reforms . . . .

There can be no doubt that this legislative act constituted the basis, indeed the birth certificate, of the Catalan parliament . . . until then there had only been . . . pre-parliamentary assemblies. The new element, as we have seen, consisted in the agreement between king and country to establish a new constitutional order for the state.

[English]

---

[1] Professor Marongiu used the word "previous," in *Il Parlamento In Italia Nel Medio Evo E Nell' Età Moderna,* cited above, p. 114, but the word does not appear in King Peter's actual concession.

9   *A Spanish Historian Discusses Counsel and Consent in the Legislation of León-Castile*

By noting the expressions which refer to the legislative activity of the Cortes, we have seen its method of operation in this field. Let us recall what was said. In the Cortes of León in 1208 we find: "I, Alfonso, . . . after much deliberation enacted this law with the agreement of all." Again, in 1188, in a Constitution about thieves and others: "by the common agreement and counsel of the barons and of my court." The Constitutions of Alfonso IX in 1194 were by common deliberation. When he communicated the Constitutions of 1194 and 1188 to the bishop of Orense, the same king declared: ". . . as we have previously enacted these things with the counsel and deliberation of the prelates and judges, and with the agreement of all our magnates, we have confirmed them by a common oath. . . ."

Two elements in these passages need to be emphasized. One reflects the consultative function of the full *Curia*. The other reflects the consent which the assembly gave to the law which was promulgated. This, together with the royal will which could be presupposed, gave the law its force. This last point has been discussed at length by students of the subject. . . . [The royal contribution is illustrated by the words of an enactment.] "An Emperor or king can make laws for the people under his lordship, and no other body must have the power to make laws about temporal matters." These words suggest an absolute ignoring of all other authority in the promulgation of laws. But in conflict with this expression of the theory of legislation are those phrases cited above in which we see not only the advice but also the agreement of members of the assembly in the promulgation of laws. Thereby, the members made a decisive contribution to the real nature of the law.

SOURCE. Nilda Guglielmi, "La Curia Regia," in *Cuadernos De Historia De España*, Vol. 28 (Instituto de Historia de España, Buenos Aires, 1958), pp. 87–89.

The problem this creates perhaps arises from a confusion between the basic theory of a supporting role in the legislative body and its practical application. We must accept the monarch's role as legislator as being among his most conspicuous attributes. In all the texts which set forth the essential features inherent in royalty we find that the right to promulgate laws has first place. Thus, in the edict of Alcalá . . . we find: "it is the prerogative of the king to make ordinances and laws, and to interpret, declare and amend them, whenever he wishes to exercise that privilege. . . . "We do not deny the validity of this concept . . . . But the practice was for the ruler to share his monarchical function with the members of the assembly. In fact, we can deduce that the legislative function of the assemblies was not only shared; it was delegated instead of being exercised by the king. Expanding and supporting the actions of the ruler, the assemblies assumed the task of legislation as their own, together with a few others which were always considered to be inherently within their capacity, and which were performed throughout the centuries.

[Spanish]

10 *French Historians Describe the Weakness of the States-General of France*

It was thus not possible in medieval France to establish a control over the royal power by either the general or the local assemblies of the nation. We may ask why and it is easy to see the answer in the case of the local assemblies. These could only act within the locality unless they obtained an agreement between all. This could not be accomplished in a country in which neither material unity nor spiritual unity [p. 577] had been achieved. On the other hand, general assemblies of all the nation were difficult to set up and to summon as long as the king did not know with any exactness what constituted his realm. Even if he had known,

SOURCE. Ferdinand Lot and Robert Fawtier, in *Histoire des Institutions Françaises*, as above, Vol. 2, pp. 576–577. Translated by permission of the Département Presses Universitaires de France, Paris, France.

could he have got his subjects to make the long journeys which would have been necessary for the delegates who attended if he had held true Estates-General? Further, could he have found a room big enough to hold the representatives of all their regions? Finally, how could the deputies of these different regions have understood each other since their speech differed? There were the languages of Langue d'Oui and of Langue d'Oc, and there was also that of Flanders; and, within each of these, appreciable differences could again make understanding difficult. It has aroused astonishment that France did not know an Estates-General whilst England had her parliament, but we do not take sufficiently into account that in the Middle Ages, France was the greatest kingdom of Europe whilst England was one of the small ones. It was necessary to wait until the unity of France was more developed before it was possible to attempt the holding of an assembly which would reflect approximately the idea of what a true States General ought to be. The point was attained in 1484. Unfortunately, it was too late.

[French]

11 The Views of Two English Historians on the Nature of the English Parliament

Now let us repeat what was said long ago, supported by a plenitude of evidence, "that parliaments are of one kind only and that, when we have stripped every non-essential away, the essence of them is the dispensing of justice by the king or by someone who in a very special sense represents the king." . . . The primary criterion by which an assembly is to be assessed is, we assert, that of function and not the presence or absence from the king's court of particular persons or some particular class of suitor. This criterion we believe to have been the contemporary criterion: the

SOURCE. H. G. Richardson and G. O. Sayles, in "Parliaments and Great Councils in Medieval England," *Law Quarterly Review*, Vol. 77 (1961), p. 407. Reprinted by permission of Associated Book Publishers Ltd and Sweet & Maxwell, London, England.

function determined whether or not a particular session of the king's council was parliament and was so termed. . . .

And since parliament was not the creation of a legislative act nor, as far as we can tell, a conscious creation at all, we cannot give a date to its inception. . . .

These two points we must emphasize. First, parliament is an afforced meeting of the council: it is an occurrence, an occasion, not yet a separate court with a continuous existence like the courts of common law. This is made clear by Henry III when he speaks of the parliament "quod habuimus cum magnatis nostris apud Oxoniam" [which we have had with our magnates at Oxford] in the summer of 1258. And secondly there are other afforced meetings of the council, not distinguishable in their constitution, which are not parliaments. We must not imagine that these two kinds of council meetings were altogether novel in 1258 and that in the Provisions of Oxford we have an act of creation. Parliaments *eo nomine*, as well as afforced councils or sessions of an afforced "great court," were already well known. . . . We believe, let us repeat, "that parliaments are of one kind only and that . . . the essence of them is the dispensing of justice. . . ."

The diffuseness of Stubbs's exposition and his neglect to resolve apparent inconsistencies between statements made in different contexts render it far from easy to form a coherent picture of the parliament of his imagination. We have done our best, by piecing together passages sometimes wide apart, to present a true and intelligible account, without, we trust, distortion or misrepresentation. This, at least, can be said: not the most ingenious of interpretations can reconcile Stubbs's conception of parliament with *Fleta*'s[2]—the conception of parliament where "the king in council holds his court in the presence of prelates, earls, barons, nobles and others learned in the law." Stubbs's parliament is not conciliar in this sense: his parliament is a national council, "the concentration of the three estates." Nor, in Stubbs's view, were the representatives of the commons on an inferior footing to the other "estates"; under Edward II, Edward III, and Richard II, he asserted, "the third estate claimed and won its place as the

2 The relevant passage is translated below, in Document 4. H. G. Richardson and G. O. Sayles have possibly overstressed one possible interpretation, in presenting their case.

foremost of the three." The picture thus presented is not one of
the English parliament of contemporary documents, not the parliament of history, but something imaginary masquerading as
history. It is, if you will, anachronistic, a projection into the past
of a "parliamentary constitution" which Stubbs believed, without
justification, to have existed in the later Middle Ages.

One of the curiosities of historiography is that, just as French
scholars have been inclined to minimize the part played by the
thirteenth-century parliament of Paris in administrative and political matters, so English scholars have tried to wish away the
judicial functions of the early English parliament. Stubbs was
nearer the truth than he imagined when he said that "the parliament of Paris [Under Philippe le Bel] may be generally compared with the special judicial session or parliament of the
council" or, again, "the point at which the two constitutions
approximated more nearly than at any other in the middle ages"
was the end of Edward I's reign in England and the reign of
Philippe le Bel in France. It may seem astonishing that Stubbs
could approach so near to the realities of history and yet persist
in his dogma of an English "parliamentary constitution," which
falsifies his teaching throughout. He could, indeed, keep himself
in countenance only by asserting that parliaments were of three
kinds and then, because the records did not bear him out, abusing
the Rolls of Parliament for their confusion.

[English]

12   The View of a Canadian Historian on the
Creation of the English Parliament

The medieval parliament, most historians would agree, developed from the feudal *Curia Regis*, with roots going back to the
Anglo-Saxon Witan. Stubbs gave it a central and essential place
in his study, and on the whole Stubbs was justified. All the politi-

SOURCE. B. Wilkinson, *The Constitutional History of Medieval England*,
Vol. 3 (London, 1958), pp. 46–49. Reprinted by permission of the Longman
Group, Harlow, England.

cal influence at work in thirteenth- and fourteenth-century England flowed together to create this great central institution which in time embraced not only the community of England but also the monarch himself. It was there that new and vital relationships were created for meeting the political challenge of that age.

Parliament offered, in point of fact, a unique meeting-place between king and community where effective co-operation in the highest matters of government could be attained; where the magnates had strong claims to such co-operation, based on custom and tradition; where the subjects could bring what was to prove a decisive pressure to bear on the expanding machine of government; and where the ancient traditions of government by counsel and consent could be given a new and more effective expression. It was, above all, the point where a new unity could be established, between the king and his subjects, to replace the informal co-operation of the feudal court; though this involved the discarding of many old notions and the acceptance of new and revolutionary ideas.

The Angevin *Curia* was dominated by feudal notions of counsel and judgement. It was in the final analysis a collection of individual vassals. It served to achieve an invaluable co-operation between the king and his tenants-in-chief; but its essential purpose was to assist the monarch in the right ordering of his affairs. Magnates had perhaps a right as well as a duty to be present; but that right did not appear as a challenge to the king's responsibility for the welfare of the realm. The *parliamentum*, on the contrary, stood in its essence for the concept of a conjoint responsibility of king and magnates. It was dominated by notions of political discussion and agreement, between the king and his subjects. It represented non-feudal relationships which were the product of a national order of politics. It transformed feudal judgement and counsel into political agreement [p. 48] and consent. Such a transformation demanded, above all, the establishment of two important concepts, neither of which was easy to achieve. The first was a new responsibility of the magnates for the welfare of the kingdom, complementary to that of the king. The second was the idea of the *universitas*, the corporate body of the magnates, far transcending in its unity of thought and action the assembly of a feudal court. Neither notion was clear-cut or fully developed in the thirteenth century; the *universitas*, in particular, was so variable and fragile that to talk of a corporate body at any time without far-reaching reservations is to be guilty of a simple distortion of the facts. Nevertheless, these twin concepts alone made possible the evolution of the thirteenth-century parliament.

The responsibility of the magnates for the kingdom was to be a matter of controversy throughout the thirteenth century. It was alien to the traditions both of feudal rights and of royal responsibilities; it was difficult to accept for both the barons and the king; and indeed its acceptance became possible only when the pressure of non-feudal relationships had weakened feudal lordship. It is not clearly stated even in Magna Carta, and not proclaimed as a principle of baronial opposition until the *Song of Lewes* and the great reform movement of 1258.

The emergence of the *universitas*, though it was merely an extension of some of the strongest feudal habits and relationships similarly encountered strong and general opposition. Henry III, who had felt the brunt of its impact, reacted strongly against it; Edward I offered an equally stubborn if less direct antagonism to some of its implications. Not only royal conservatism had to be overcome; for feudal individualism was strong, and the royal determination to deal with individuals and not a *universitas* was hard to resist. Robert Grosseteste's admonition to the prelates in 1244 is not to be dismissed as mere rhetoric: "Do not let us be divided from the common counsel," he urged, "for it is written that if we shall be divided, immediately we shall all perish"; and there is no doubt that the barons as well as the prelates needed such advice. In 1242, Henry III tried to persuade his barons one at a time to aid him, interviewing them in his private chamber, as Matthew Paris observed, "in the manner of penitents before a priest." The magnates might take an oath to give a common reply, or to do nothing without the general *universitas*; but it is evident from such acts that a common front did not come easily. In 1255, Henry bound some of the leading magnates to his side so as to impede the *universitas regni* in standing for its rights; and in December of that year, Matthew censured them for going home, each man to take his own counsel "in the manner of Englishmen." . . .

[English]

CHAPTER IV

THE BEGINNINGS OF REPRESENTATION

The importance of the adoption of representation has always been recognized. As Professor Helen Cam has said,[1] "Though representation is an old, not to say hackneyed subject, we can never get away from it. It is the basis of our Anglo-American assumptions about democracy, though unknown to the Greeks who invented the word . . . and repudiated by Rousseau, the prophet of modern democracy." Professor Cam might have gone further and claimed that it is the basis of the practice of modern democracy as well as of our assumptions about it. Without representation, modern democracy could not have been achieved, in spite of some modern claims to the contrary.

In one sense, as Professor H. M. Cam argued, representation of merchants and others in parliament alongside the magnates was a natural development: long before jurists and scholastics began examining the bearing of the word representation, the thing itself was already on the scene as an obvious common sense solution to constantly recurring problems. Just as the rise of the territorial state brought about the creation of the first parliaments by king and magnates, the development of royal justice brought about the inclusion of representatives. It was all very simple and inevitable.

But in point of fact, the process was neither simple nor inevitable. It changed the nature of the parliamentary assembly from being essentially feudal into being essentially non-feudal, or at least as representing a mixture of feudal and non-feudal ideas. It

---

[1] "The Theory and Practice of Representation in Medieval England," in *History*, Vol. 38 (Feb., 1953), pp. 11–26; reprinted in *Lawfinders and Lawmakers in Medieval England* (London, 1963), pp. 159–175.

created new and complex problems of political alignment, and especially of the relationship of the new arrivals to the monarch and to the magnates. And, just as the earliest parliaments were the product of a long and complex process of evolution, so was the inclusion of the citizens and others. It represented a journey every bit as remarkable as that which the magnates had made, and in some respects more difficult. After all, the great men had always had a tradition of cooperation with the king at the summit, but this had not been shared by humbler people, despite the vigour of their regional and local life.

It is impossible to trace the development of representation in any detail. In Spain the beginnings in the Cortes go back beyond the famous assembly of 1188; in England King John in 1213 summoned four discreet knights from each county to speak with him at Oxford "about the business of our kingdom"; and in Germany Emperor Frederick II summoned citizens as early as 1231. The very act of summons was itself deeply significant. It heralded the arrival of a new political force in the old assembly of the magnates and the king. And it was followed by the acquisition by some representatives of full power to bind their constituents (if we may use a modern word), the so-called *plena potestas*, which owed a good deal to the revived study of Roman Law. Procurators who had such power were elected in Spain as early as 1223. Nevertheless, all this was only a beginning. Whether they had full power or not, the representatives only became an important factor in the parliamentary assembly when they followed the path marked out by the nobles before them and acquired some recognized right to agree to important acts of the king, as well as the right to be informed and to acclaim. It was only then that they began to exercise a significant influence, and in some countries began to change the very nature of parliament.

The assemblies of Spain pointed the way. But in spite of that they were not, as is often argued, the true pioneers in the parliamentary revolution caused by the advent of the commoners. This was not because they were denied genuine participation in the Cortes, but rather because, as suggested above, the Cortes itself did not quite fulfil its early promise of achieving rule by agreement between the subjects and the king. What the magnates themselves did not accomplish obviously could not be attained by the representatives.

Citizens were, indeed, prominent in the Spanish assemblies. They were summoned to the notable Cortes of 1188.[2] They were present when king Alfonso IX was said to have promulgated a law in favour of the church in an assembly at León, called during February 1208. The law was enacted after much deliberation with the consent of everyone. Citizens were prominent in the acclamation of new kings and on similar occasions. The "good men of Castile and León" were consulted by Fernando III in 1250, and the King said that he had summoned the men of the towns to discuss matters touching the good estate of the realm.

The citizens of Spain were exceptionally important because of the key role they played in the wars against the Moors and the settlement of conquered towns; but the cautious words of Professor J. O'Callaghan quoted below show that they were slow to change their early right to counsel and acclaim into a more challenging right to agreement. It is even doubtful if they established a right of consent to the levy of special taxes. Professor O'Callaghan says of Castile-León, "No doubt the monarchy found it convenient to summon the townsmen to the great council for many reasons: to inquire into the administration of the municipalities, to adjudicate their lawsuits, to seek their counsel in military affairs, and to obtain their financial assistance."[3] But, as he says, the king remained the central and predominant figure. He sought counsel and discussion, but he was not bound to seek agreement. And it will be noticed that O'Callaghan has nothing to say about the right of the townsmen to "treat" about important matters; they had no status comparable to that achieved by their counterparts in England, even though León seems to have developed the idea of "treaty" more fully, perhaps, than any other kingdom in Spain.

The presence of the citizens was not, in fact, all gain for the future of the Cortes. While on the one hand it made the Spanish kingdoms more "democratic," on the other it may have helped pave the way for despotism. It has been observed that on the whole the development of the communes in Spain gave political importance to an element which was opposed to the nobles; that

[2] See Chapter II, and *ibid.*, Documents 6 and 7. ·

[3] "The Beginnings of the Cortes of León-Castile," in *A.H.R.* Vol. 74 (June, 1969), p. 1533.

was one reason why it was favored by the kings. But while a policy of opposing and weakening the nobles was in many ways beneficial, it weakened one of the most important restraints on the power of the ruler and thus strengthened the tendency towards absolute rule.

In Germany and Sicily, the situation was not very different. Rulers there set important precedents for the presence of representatives at meetings of the general *Curia*, both of the Empire and in the princely states. As in almost every other country, the importance of citizens and others was now so great that they could not be excluded entirely from such gatherings. But Henry VII, whose Edict of 1231 has been discussed above, seems to have wanted to use them mainly as a restraint on the lords; he was much less influenced by the principle of consent, though it had obviously found wide acceptance. Otherwise he could not have invoked it in such an important pronouncement as this.

His father did not have to fear the magnates in the same way; but the idea of strengthening his position by the loyalty and support of representatives may not have been entirely absent from his mind. It is not likely, however, that he dreamt of a genuine partnership with them in the weighty affairs of his realm. Henry VII himself, as we have seen, destroyed much of the effectiveness of the representatives as a brake on the prince; he only gave the "better men" a right to agree beforehand that the prince should legislate. The German tradition was quite compatible with the summoning of citizens and others; but it nevertheless militated against their achievement of a genuine partnership in legislation. No king in Europe was anxious to share power with the humble commoners, but on the whole German Emperors and princes were probably more reluctant than most.

Despite this, ideas of representation persisted among them. In 1254, William of Holland, King of the Romans, promised that both lords and cities should send four "solemn messengers" (*sollempnes nuncios*), to future assemblies, with full power. In 1255, the royal confirmation of the great confederation of Rhenish cities was made with the unanimous consent of nobles and citizens. There is little doubt that William's desperate need for support made him turn to the powerful cities and strengthen their representation in the Imperial Diet. Had William not met an unfortunate death in January, 1256, his weakness and his needs might just possibly have led to a dramatic development. But the princes were against the cities; just as they opposed an enlargement of Imperial power, they did not wish to see the ruler and the people come closer together in the Imperial Diet.

In the confusion which followed William's death, the possibility of development which his policy had opened up was effectively destroyed. The history of Germany shows how much more was needed to create a strong and enduring representation than royal expediency. Representation which would create the possibility of a future democracy demanded favourable conditions in the community as well as support from the king, and the varied history of the local assemblies in Germany reflects the diversity of local influences and traditions which influenced their growth.[4]

It was in England, among the more important states, that the idea of such a partnership was in the end most successfully established, though not without great difficulty and friction. The ground had been prepared, as we have seen, during centuries when cooperation between king and magnates had been steadily developed. The idea of the expansion of such cooperation to include also citizens and others was made easier to accept by the importance of knights and burgesses in the shires and hundreds, where they had practiced "self government at the king's command" since Anglo-Saxon days. The conditions were strongly favourable to an expanding participation of this "middling" element in the work of the central, as well as the local, government. If this could not be achieved in England, it was not very likely to be achieved in any other major country of the West.

Such a partnership had been brought an important step further by Magna Carta. This was essentially the creation of the magnates; but their success had been aided by sympathy from Englishmen of all ranks; and this pointed the way to a closer association of lords and commoners in future opposition to their ruler. The result was that the barons who acted against Henry III claimed increasingly to stand for the whole community of England, including knights of the shire and burgesses; and it was natural that when they broke into open revolt and sought to use parliament as an instrument of reform they should include in it the commoners who gave them support. Thus, representation in

[4] For Frederick II in Apulia, see Document 1.

England was imposed on the ruler rather than adopted by him for his own ends. It reflected an exceptionally strong association of all the politically articulate classes. There was a balance in the country which made it impossible for the king to exclude the knights and burgesses from the parliamentary assembly, even though their participation was very limited for many years. These beginnings were decisive. Indeed, the stamp which they impressed on the English parliament has never been erased.

Of course, representation was not only a matter of politics. Justice and taxation both played an important role; and it is probably true to say that the main purpose for which the commoners were willing to bear the burden of attendance was that of obtaining justice at the hands of the king or the council at the time of parliament. Taxation was similarly of supreme importance. It was more and more a non-feudal levy on all people of substance; and the principle of consent that we may see in Magna Carta applied with increasing clarity to others besides tenants-in-chief. In 1225 it was declared that in return for the reissue of the Charter the magnates, the knights, the freeholders, and all the realm had granted the king a tax. As Sir Maurice Powicke pointed out, the idea that taxation was a personal affair, so that one man could agree and another refuse, was overcome by the conception of action by the community. Within this conception was the germ of representation, for only by virtue of it could all the community act.

Inevitably, such a development created a danger that the freemen of England might be regarded as being represented by the lords. As Miss Maude Clarke long ago suggested, the king and the magnates might have acted together to render nugatory the consent of the subtenants, and probably of the freemen as well. The great lords might have thus secured for themselves a permanent exemption from taxation, as happened in some countries of Europe. It seems likely, however, that Miss Clarke exaggerated this particular danger, though her suggestion serves to warn us not to take the triumph of representation and the rise of the Commons in England for granted. Both may be described without much exaggeration as virtually miraculous. They could only be achieved in a moment of precarious political balance, and they were the outcome of an evolution which has been regarded as unique.

Representation in England may be taken as accepted for some purposes in 1254 when, during the absence of the king, two knights were summoned from each shire to come before the king's council of regency to discuss the granting of an aid. Some years before this, in 1232, a grant had been recorded as being made by the magnates, freeholders, and villeins, but we do not know how this agreement was obtained. The writ of summons of 1254 did indeed establish representation; but the knights were only summoned before the council, in the king's absence abroad, in order to "provide . . . what short of aid they will give us." Henry III was not very different in his attitude towards royal authority from the rulers of Spain. What changed the situation in England was not so much the wishes of the king as the purposes and needs of the barons, hostile to the growing power of central government.

Driven both by their necessities and their ideals, the magnates acting in opposition to their ruler, caused representatives of the shires to be summoned to parliament, to "treat" about the common affairs of the kingdom; and it is conclusive proof of the significance of the language used that Henry countermanded this particular summons and directed the knights to appear before him, and not before the barons, and not to "treat," but only to have a colloquy with the king.[5] In 1264 and 1265, during great crises, the opposition to Henry repeated the summons to treat, and this form of summons became customary in spite of the royalist restoration after 1265. Thus, in England, the barons "allied" themselves with the representatives, and helped to give them a position in parliament comparable with, if greatly inferior, to that which they had obtained for themselves.

The consequences for England may perhaps be illustrated by a brief reference to a famous tag from the laws of the Emperor Justinian, which was often quoted in the Middle Ages and is frequently discussed by historians at the present day. It is brief and pithy—*Quod omnes tangit ab omnibus approbetur*—(what touches all should be approved by all). But, like almost everything else that pertains to the medieval parliament, its significance is a matter of debate. It seems to be quite certain that Justinian's lawyers did not believe that it put the Emperor under an ob-

[5] Document 2.

ligation to get agreement from his subjects for important acts, at least not formal consent in an assembly. Approval might take many forms and might at times become nothing more than acclamation. It is hard to know exactly what Frederick II had in mind when he used the phrase in inviting the lay and ecclesiastical princes of the Empire to Verona in 1244 to discuss what was necessary in order to reestablish good relations with the Church, and when he commented further that he wished to avail himself of the counsel and assent of the princes in so solemn and serious a matter. It is unlikely, on the whole, that he thought of himself as laying down a general principle of government by consent. On the other hand, it obviously could mean just that, and there is a strong suspicion that it did when the English chronicler Matthew Paris, whose sympathies were strongly with the baronial opposition to Henry III, translated it to mean that what concerns all ought to be *treated about* as well as approved by all. And it may have meant the same when King Edward I used it in a famous summons of the prelates and lower clergy to the "model" parliament of 1295; he added that it was very evident, from this precept, that common dangers should be met by remedies provided in common (*communiter*). English experience gave the tag a significance different from that to be found in the Imperial tradition. *Quod omnes tangit* expressed the English interpretation, established by great struggles and debates, and probably accepted, subject always to his own paternalistic concept of his office, by even the masterful Edward I. If there was any doubt, it was removed by his enforced acceptance of the Confirmation of the Charters in 1297. In this, the king promised not to levy certain important taxes except by "the common assent of the whole kingdom," and not to impose extra customs on wool except with the "common assent and good will" of those who had felt themselves to be oppressed by this particular tax. Here was a practical and striking application of the principle that what touches all shall be approved by all.

Thus an effective balance was struck in thirteenth century England between the king and the community of the realm; including what we may call the middling classes. There was no such balance in contemporary France where, as suggested above, the monarchy made impressive gains. Despite this, the French king Philip the Fair summoned the famous States-General of 1302

which included many burgesses. We have already seen that these
played an important part in the assembly,[6] and the writs which
summoned them made it clear that they were intended to do so.[7]
Like the nobles, they were summoned to "treat"; but they were
also directed to come prepared to receive and to do, and to consent without any excuse to what should be ordained. The king
(apparently the king only) was to ordain. There was a world of
difference between the status of the French burgesses in this assembly and that of the English burgesses and knights in the age
of Simon de Montfort and Edward I. The burgesses played a
striking role in the States-General of 1302; but their presence
did not permanently change the political balance in the general
assembly or lead to an eventual sovereignty of king lords and
commons on the model of the English parliament.

Nor was this simply because of the greater distance which
separated the French lords and commoners as compared with
the English. As Professor Russell Major argues, "the line between
noble and non-noble was so vague as almost to defy definition,"
and:

"A deputy to the estates-general was usually elected and em-
powered by all three estates, but even when named by a single
order of society, local ties bound him as strongly to the other
orders of his community as his class bound him to members of
his estate from other parts of France . . . he represented a particular region whose privileges and autonomy he was carefully
instructed to maintain."[8]

The pattern of 1302 was continued in later years; and the
burgesses, led by Etienne Marcel, even assumed a dominant role
in the assembly in 1346 and 1347, during the crisis of the Hundred Years War; but their efforts aroused the strong opposition of
both the monarch and the nobles, and they very quickly petered
out. This underlines perhaps the greatest weakness of representation in the States-General. It began as the product of royal
needs and policy, adopted to meet a great crisis in foreign affairs.
The representatives were to be the instruments of the king. They

[6] Chapter III.

[7] Document 4.

[8] *The Estates-General of 1560* (Princeton University Press, 1951) pp. 73–75.

could only change this role by an "alliance" with the magnates which they failed to obtain. As in Germany, they might have developed significant powers if circumstances had not turned against the whole parliamentary experiment. The English helped to destroy the success of this experiment by the same military aggression which, ironically, helped to ensure its final success in England herself. But in truth the basis for either success or failure in both countries had been laid long before the Hundred Years War.

The most important causes, in every country alike, are to be found in general conditions rather than in particular events, though we must never underestimate the influence of individuals like Philip the Fair or Simon de Montfort. Representation was the unique European response to a unique set of circumstances, combined with age-long traditions of individual dignity (in the aristocracy), individual rights, limited authority, and collective action, however rudimentary. The assertion of these traditions against the growing claims of state-power was inevitable; but a "coalition" with the citizens and others to defend them was not. It did not happen in Germany and France. The reason why it happened in England was probably that the lords were defending, and were known to be defending, the ancient political traditions as well as their own privileges, even though the two were hard to separate. They received the general support of knights and burgesses, and in turn they helped to establish representation. Representation supported liberty; but only where it was itself sustained by the magnates rather than by the king. Where it was nothing more than a royal expedient, it was a threat to freedom rather than the reverse.

To say this is not to ignore the selfish attachment to privilege by both barons and burghers. This was universal. In any medieval parliament there was much talk of privileges and rarely talk of freedom. But to a medieval man the two tended to be inseparable. Privileges were an important bulwark against absolute power. But their defense did not necessarily result in representation, much less in the integration of the representatives into parliament. Success in this depended on many factors, some affecting the communities of the localities, some affecting the barons. With regard to the former, it needed not only traditions of self-government in the localities, such as were found abundantly in the European *communes*, but also a strong habit of cooperation by the men of the localities with the work of the central government. In England, this existed, especially in the field of justice. But representation did not grow simply out of a transference to the supreme court of parliament of the ideas and practices of the local courts. It grew out of the expanding economic and political importance of the local communities, great enough to bring their representatives into parliament, but not great enough, even in England, to give them a secure position there without baronial support.

The success of representation needed a willingness, on the part of the magnates, to recognize a measure of identity between their aims and those of the commonalty. This could only be achieved if they concentrated less on the defense of privileges, which they did not share with the local communities, and more on the defense of a common freedom from undue exploitation by the Crown, in which all had a concern. Their attitude was, in fact, a good deal more important than that of the ruler which was largely predetermined. It is true that the kings initiated representation; it was brought into being by their writs of summons and to this extent reflected royal policy. But it is probable that no king was enthusiastic about it, except on terms which would destroy its vitality. Most of them probably recognized the authenticity of the tradition expressed in Justinian's *Quod omnes tangit*; but they tried to reconcile it with the preservation, and even with the extension, of their authority. Both circumstances and their own human nature made them cling to expanding powers even though these were clearly one cause of friction and violence in the state, and even though rulers like Frederick II must have perceived that a new spirit was abroad in the land.

The ultimate fate of representation was, in consequence, decided by the aristocracy; by whether they could, or could not, combine with the expanding force of the citizens and the less important gentry. This was a supreme challenge, and both traditions and circumstances were against them. Their privileges generally mattered more to them than the common good. Their history was closely bound up with the idea of a unique position at the side of the ruler. His power was in a sense theirs, and his glory was reflected upon them. They were too long accustomed to regard the "men of work" as unfitted to share in the supreme management of affairs. Hence it is not surprising that in countries like Germany and France, in spite of aristocratic opposition to the growing power of the ruler, the magnates failed to make common cause with members of the lower estates. Even in England, their success in this respect was in some ways a defiance of the law of political gravity.

It must be repeated that the whole experiment of representation, on the scale practiced in the West, was a unique phenomenon; its successful outcome, even in a limited area, changed the course of history. If England, favoured to an exceptional degree, was the only great state to achieve conspicuous success, this should not surprise us. In any case, all the other states shared in the common effort, and carried on into modern times the traditions and memories of this exceptional age. Modern representation was never a complete innovation, but only a revival. And England provided both an example and a stimulus. Before the end of the Middle Ages, the English had included representatives in a new kind of "sovereignty," that of the king-in-parliament. Through this conjoint "sovereignty" (the word was not used in the modern sense during the Middle Ages) the government could be made ever stronger without the king becoming despotic. Order could be indefinitely expanded in the state without the loss of liberty. As Henry VIII would proclaim in the sixteenth century:

"We be informed by our judges that we at no time stand so high in our estate royal as in the time of parliament, when we as head and you [the Lords and Commons] are conjoined and knit together in one body politic."

Thus, representation created a concept of government which led straight to modern democracy. The obscure experiments and conflicts of parliament's early beginnings were the prelude to one of the most majestic, if at the same time most fragile, experiments in political life that has been recorded in the history of civilized man.

1   *A Summons by Frederick II of the Better Men*
      from Cities and Castles, to an Assembly
              at Foggia in 1232

In the month of September, the Emperor came from Melfi to
Foggia, and directed general letters throughout all the kingdom,
directing that two of the better men should come to him from
each city or castle for the utility of the realm and the common
good.
[Latin]

SOURCE. From the *Chronica de Ryccardi de Sancto Germano*, edited by
Carlo Alberto Garufi, in *Rerum Italicarum Scriptores: Raccolta Degli Storici
Italiani* (Bologna, 1936-8) Vol. 7, part 2, p. 183. The author was an expert,
a public notary, used to meticulous wording. He had just recorded an important pronouncement by the Emperor in which Frederick arranged for a
"treating" (*tractatus*) between prelate and magnates as part of a settlement
of peace with the Church. If the "treating" failed, the questions at issue
were to go to arbitration. This was in 1230 (ibid., p. 168). Thus the words
Ryccardi used in describing the summons of the better men in 1232 become
very significant.

2   *Summons of Knights of the Shire to an*
              English Assembly in 1261

The king to the sheriff of Norfolk and Suffolk greeting.
Whereas on the part of the bishop of Worcester, the earl of
Leicester, the earl of Gloucester, and certain other nobles of
our realm, three knights have been summoned from each of our
counties to be at St. Albans on the approaching feast of St.
Matthew the Apostle, in order with them to treat about (*tractare*)
the common affairs of our kingdom and whereas we and our

SOURCE. Printed in Stubbs's *Select Charters*, from the *Report on the Dignity
of a Peer* (London, 1820–29), Vol. 3, translated by B. Wilkinson, *Constitutional
History 1215–1399*, as above, pp. 303–304. Reprinted by permission of the
Longman Group, Harlow, England.

nobles aforesaid shall come together on the same day at Windsor to treat concerning peace between us and them; we command you on our part to give strict orders to those knights from your bailiwick, who have been summoned before those nobles on the aforesaid day, the avoiding all excuse they come to us at Windsor on the said day (and you are also strictly to prohibit them from going elsewhere on that day) to have a conference (*colloquium*) with us on the aforesaid matters; so that, as a consequence of this business, they may see and understand that we propose no undertaking but what we know to be for the honour and common benefit of our realm. By witness of the king at Windsor, September 11.

[Latin]

3   *Summons of Knights of the Shire to a Montfortian Parliament in June, 1264*

The king to Adam of Newmarket greeting. Whereas the disturbance recently experienced in our kingdom has now subsided and, by the grace of divine co-operation, peace has now been ordained and established between us and our barons; and whereas, in order that this peace may be inviolably observed throughout our entire kingdom, it has been provided by the counsel and assent of our barons that in each of our counties throughout England keepers of our peace shall be appointed for the defence and security of those parts . . . and whereas in our approaching parliament it is necessary for us to "treat" with our prelates, magnates and other faithful men concerning our affairs and those of our kingdom: we command you to send to us on behalf of the entire county aforesaid four of the more lawful and discreet knights of the same county, elected for that purpose by the assent

SOURCE. Printed in Stubbs's *Select Charters*, pp. 399–400, from Rymer's *Foedera*, Vol. I p. 442, translated by B. Wilkinson in *Constitutional History 1216–1399*, as above, p. 304. Reprinted by permission of the Longman Group, Harlow, England.

of that county; so that they will be with us at London on the octave of the approaching feast of the Holy Trinity at the latest, in order to "treat" with us on the aforesaid affairs . . . . By witness of the king at St. Paul's in London, June 4.

[Latin]

4   *Summons of Burgesses to the French*
          States-General of 1302

Philip, by the grace of God king of the French, to the seneschal of Carcassonne or his lieutenant, greeting. We wish to deliberate and treat with the prelates, barons, and other faithful men and subjects of ours and of the realm, on many and weighty matters. These greatly concern us and the estate and liberty of us and of our realm; also those of the churches, the clergy, the nobles, the secular persons, and the singular and universal inhabitants of our same realm. We therefore command the consuls and *universitates* of Narbonne . . . , by the fealty and by whatever bond they are held fast to us, as follows. The said consuls and *universitates* of the cities and towns aforesaid shall be present at Paris in the person of two or three of the great and wiser of each *universitas* aforesaid. These shall have full and express power among other things from the aforesaid consuls and *universitates* to hear, to receive, and to do, all and singular matters, and to consent without any excuse . . . to all and singular which shall be ordained by us in this matter . . . . They shall be present in Paris [on a certain day] to treat and to deliberate on these matters: to hear, to receive and to do all and singular and to offer assent, their own and in the name of the consuls and *universitates* aforesaid, all and singular, to what shall be obtained by us regarding the foregoing which touch them . . . .

SOURCE. C. H. Taylor, "Some New Texts on the Assembly of 1302," in *Speculum*, Vol. 11 (1936), pp. 38–42. Translated by B. Wilkinson, by permission of the Medieval Academy of America. Cambridge, Mass. U.S.A.

CONCLUSION

One or two obvious conclusions seem to follow from this survey, together with others not so obvious. The underlying unity of the development of medieval parliaments has already been stressed, but it is worth pointing out that such unity is almost as evident in the case of the representatives as in that of the magnates. Second, it is worth repeating that the whole process was no accident or freak of history. It was the expression of certain ideas which were at the very heart of feudal society. Third, however, it was also the product of what in terms of the historian's outlook may be called a fleeting moment of balance, of political equilibrium, between the ruler and the subjects, which enabled men to translate the somewhat primitive processes of early feudalism into the practices of the more advanced territorial state. It was fortunate that in this moment of balance, Roman concepts of authority were still outweighed by Teutonic traditions and feudal customs, both of which were on the side of limited power. Hence, men did not attempt a short cut in seeking to solve the problems of the territorial state by recourse only to the authority of the prince; though the tendency to extol this authority often triumphed in the end.

Modern historians, as already suggested, still differ widely as to the nature of the early parliament and the causes of its creation, and the same is true of representation. It has been impossible to do justice to these differences of opinion or to examine the evolution of parliament in each country of the West. But enough has emerged from a glance at the highlights of the process to suggest the interest we may still find in the analysis made long ago by Stubbs, which is printed below.[1] Stubbs may have been

[1] Document 1.

somewhat insular, and he may have believed, as Professor Marongiu suggests, that it was the mission of the English to create a parliamentary regime. But, as the same writer truly says, if the bishop was not the first, he was certainly the greatest English parliamentary historian. His summary of European developments is remarkable, short though it is, even though its brevity prevented an adequate indication of the importance which must be attributed to the early contributions of Italy and Spain.

Perhaps enough has been said to suggest that approach to the problem of parliamentary origins should be in the spirit of Otto Hintze and Antonio Marongiu rather than that of the English historians Richardson and Sayles. It takes away much of the significance of a great institution to define it at any point as only a court set above other courts, however important we regard its judicial functions. Such a view tends to obscure the fact that parliament was the outcome of a whole way of life, sustained by political ideas which were, and still are, of paramount importance.

The debt we owe to the pioneers of parliamentary government is incalculable. Nothing has ever been found to replace the parliamentary process in the government of a large territorial state, though this should not be taken to suggest that nothing ever will. No means have been discovered to serve better the reconciliation of liberty and authority in the complicated structure of the modern state. It is not too much to say that, without parliament, the powers placed in the hands of the ruler in the thirteenth century would have borne all the kings of Europe irresistibly on the path to absolute power. Even as it was, political liberty was only with great difficulty preserved. Without parliament and without liberty, it is improbable that European civilization would have continued to progress, or that we should still continue, though somewhat precariously, to enjoy both order and liberty at the present day.

Much still remains to be discovered, and many obvious problems are still to be more deeply probed. In particular, the whole evolution of the general assembly of magnates and the development in it of counsel and agreement, instead of merely counsel, has yet to be fully explored. As will have already become evident, the investigation of this and of many other problems is, indeed, being vigorously pursued. One of the most striking phenomena of historical study in the last forty years has been the burgeoning interest in the study of parliament and the broadening concept of its place in history. We owe a sincere tribute in particular to the pioneers of the International Commission for the History of Representative and Parliamentary Institutions. It is sometimes said that institutions are most studied in any community when they have passed their point of greatest utility; but this is almost certainly not true of parliament. It seems more likely that the modern researches have been stimulated by the challenge of some modern doctrines and the dilemma presented by the twentieth century explosion of bureaucracy. It seems almost beyond question that they will help towards a deeper understanding of the society which created the medieval parliament and of the ideas and sources of strength that helped to produce such creativeness and such remarkable growth.

1   *Stubbs on the Development of Parliaments in Europe*

The idea of a constitution in which each class of society should, as soon as it was fitted for the trust, be admitted to a share of power and control, and in which national action should be determined by the balance maintained between the forces thus combined, never perhaps presented itself to the mind of any medieval politician. The shortness of life, and the jealousy inherent in and attendant on power, may account for this in the case of the practical statesman, although a long reign like that of Henry III might have given room for the experiment; and, whilst a strong feeling of jealousy subsisted throughout the middle ages between the king and the barons, there was no such strong feeling between the barons and the commons.

But even the scholastic writers, amid their calculations of all possible combinations of principles in theology and morals, well aware of the difference between the *rex politicus* who rules according to law and the tyrant who rules without it, and of

SOURCE. W. Stubbs, *The Constitutional History of England* (Fourth edition, reprinted, Oxford, 1906) Vol. 2, pp. 167–169.

the characteristics of monarchy, aristocracy and democracy, with their respective corruptions, contented themselves for the most part with balancing the spiritual and secular powers, and never broached the idea of a growth into political enfranchisement. Yet, in the long run, this has been the ideal towards which the healthy development of national life in Europe has constantly tended, only the steps towards it have not been taken to suit a preconceived theory. The immediate object in each case has been to draw forth the energy of the united people in some great emergency, to suit the convenience of party or the necessities of kings, to induce the newly admitted classes to give their money, to produce political contentment, or to involve all alike in the consciousness of common responsibility.

The history of the thirteenth century fully illustrates this. Notwithstanding the difference of circumstances and the variety of results, it is to this period that we must refer, in each country of Europe, the introduction, or the consolidation, for the first time since feudal principles forced their way into the machinery of government, of national assemblies composed of properly arranged and organized Estates. The accepted dates in some instances fall outside the century. The first recorded appearance of town representation in the Cortes of Aragon is placed in 1162; the first in Castile in 1169. The general courts of Frederick II in Sicily were framed in 1232: in Germany the cities appear by deputies in the diet of 1255, but they only began to form a distinct part under Henry VII and Lewis of Bavaria; in France the States General are called together first in 1302. Although in each case the special occasions differ, the fact, that a similar expedient was tried in all, shows that the class to which recourse was for the first time had was in each country rising in the same or in a proportional degree, or that the classes which had hitherto monopolised power were in each country feeling the need of a reinforcement. The growth of the towns in wealth and strength, and the decline of properly feudal ideas in kings, clergy and barons, tended to the momentary parallelism. The way in which the crisis was met decided in each country the current of history. In England the parliamentary system of the middle ages emerged from the policy of Henry II, Simon de Montfort and Edward I; in France the States General were so managed as to place the whole realm under royal absolutism; in Spain the long struggle ended in the sixteenth century in making the king despotic, but the failure of the constitution arose directly from the fault of its original structure. The Sicilian policy of Frederick passed away with his house. In Germany the disruption of all central government was reflected in the Diet; the national paralysis showed itself in a series of abortive attempts, few and far between, at united action, and the real life was diverted into provincial channels and dynastic designs.

A NOTE ON BIBLIOGRAPHY

An introduction to the vast literature on the subject is to be found in the survey by H. M. Cam, A. Marongiu, and G. Stökl, "Recent Work and Present Views on the Origin and Development of the Representative Assemblies," in *Relazioni del Congresso Internazionale di Scienze Storiche* (Florence, 1955), pp. 3–101. There are references to many modern publications in A. Marongiu's *Il Parlamento in Italia Nel Medio Evo E Nell' Età Moderna,* (Milan, 1962), published as Volume 25 in *Studies Presented to the International Commission for the History of Representative and Parliamentary Institutions.* It has been adapted and translated by S. J. Woolf, under the title of *Medieval Parliaments, a Comparative Study,* and equipped with a bibliography (London, 1968). There is much bibliographical information in the numerous publications of the *International Commission for the History of Representative and Parliamentary Institutions.* A list of the *Studies Presented to the International Commission* is printed in Volume 24—*Album Helen Maud Cam* (Louvain, 1961). See also A. R. Myers, "Parliaments in Europe: the Representative Tradition," in *History To-Day,* Vol. 5. (1955), pp. 383–390, 446–454; R. S. Hoyt, "Recent Publications in the United States and Canada on the History of Western Representative Institutions before the French Revolution," *Speculum,* Vol. 29 (April, 1954), pp. 356–377; and a good popular survey, by P. Bodet, *Early English Parliaments* (Boston, 1968).